What Is Wrong With Scientology?

Healing through Understanding

Mark 'Marty' Rathbun

Copyright © 2012 Mark Rathbun

All rights reserved.

ISBN: 1477453466
ISBN-13: 978-1477453469

LCCN: 2012910574

For Monique -

who healed me and helps me to heal others.

ABOUT THE AUTHOR

Mark "Marty" Rathbun was Inspector General of the Religious Technology Center (RTC), the organization that controls the copyrights and trademarks of the materials relating to Dianetics and Scientology. His role was to head the Inspector General Network, described by the Church of Scientology as "an independent investigatory and policing body whose function is to keep Scientology working by ensuring the pure and ethical use of Dianetics and Scientology technology." The post is one of the most senior management functions in the Church and its related organizations.

Rathbun left the Church of Scientology in 2004. He is now an independent Scientologist. As such he and his wife, Monique, provide counseling and auditing services for other Scientologists that have cut their ties with the Church of Scientology. He emerged as a critical source in a 2009 St. Petersburg Times expose on the organization, revealing that physical violence is a common occurrence within Scientology management, and that Scientology head David Miscavige regularly beats his staff and orders staff to administer beatings to designated individuals. The series by the Times titled "Inside Scientology: The Truth Rundown" (http://tinyurl.com/mjcnfv) was recognized with honors including the 2010 Gold Medal for Public Service award from the Florida Society of News Editors, and was a finalist for the 2010 National Headliner Awards in the category of investigative reporting.

Rathbun has also been profiled by the following publications:

The UK Independent: http://tinyurl.com/cwahwzy
Texas Monthly magazine: http://tinyurl.com/758rb75
The Village Voice: http://tinyurl.com/5tjnhuc
Rathbun operates a blog called Moving On Up a Little Higher: markrathbun.wordpress.com

THE EDITORS

I had the good fortune of having two of the most competent and qualified people in the world edit this book on Scientology. In addition to knowing just about all there is to know about the subject they both are great writers and editors.

Dan Koon

Dan was introduced to Scientology in 1969 at the Berkeley California Scientology Mission. He joined staff there in 1971. Between 1974 and 1976 he audited to the state of Clear and trained through the St Hill Special Briefing Course (an intensive two to three year study of all lectures and writings covering the entire development of Dianetics and Scientology) at an advanced Scientology organization in Los Angeles. In 1977 Dan joined the Sea Organization (Scientology's priesthood) and was stationed at Scientology's international headquarters for the next twenty-seven years. He worked directly with Scientology Founder L. Ron Hubbard on technical training films produced to help perfect the art and science of Scientology counseling. He spent thirteen years as a senior researcher and writer for the L. Ron Hubbard Technical Compilations Unit. That group searched, organized and compiled Hubbard's Scientology writings in accordance with Hubbard's written wishes. Dan left the organization in December 2003 when after years of deteriorating liberties it had taken on the character of an insular cult. Dan is a painter and writer. He also continues to consult independent Scientology practitioners. He lives with his wife Mariette in her native Sweden.

Russell Williams

Russ got involved in Scientology in 1974 in Phoenix Arizona. He joined the Sea Organization in early 1975 and served for the next thirty years. For the first seven years Russ held a wide variety of posts directly involved with the delivery of Scientology training and auditing. During the 80s and early 90s, Russ worked in the Hubbard Technical Compilations Unit – along with Dan Koon, for several of those years. During the early 80s Russ corresponded regularly with L. Ron Hubbard, coordinating the compilations of Hubbard's work into books, reference volumes, and course packs. In the mid-90s, Russ worked for a stint in Scientology's international management, as the highest authority over the delivery of Scientology services. Finally, after spending several years in a Scientology concentration camp (described in more detail in this book) Russ decided his dignity and integrity required he break ties with Scientology Inc. In 2004 he moved back to Phoenix, where he works as a freelance writer, editor and photographer, consults independent Scientologists, and enjoys life.

COVER ART AND DESIGN

By Evelyn Cook.

ART AND DESIGN EDITING

By Renere Lopez

CONTENTS

	Introduction	Pg. 1
1	What is Scientology?	Pg. 7
2	Black Dianetics	Pg. 21
3	Training	Pg. 29
4	Rudiments	Pg. 39
5	Objectives	Pg. 45
6	Grades	Pg. 51
7	Confessional	Pg. 59
8	Ethics	Pg. 67
9	Suppression	Pg. 79
10	Right and Wrong	Pg. 93
11	Clear	Pg. 105
12	Differentiation	Pg. 113
13	Reversal	Pg. 121
14	OT Levels	Pg. 131
15	Hereafter	Pg. 141
16	Purpose	Pg. 155

Mark Rathbun

INTRODUCTION

When actor and former prominent Scientologist Jason Beghe spoke out about abuses of the church of Scientology, he pulled no punches. Beghe's 2008 exit interview with journalist Mark Bunker went viral on YouTube. Fresh from emerging out of twelve years of a personal living hell, Beghe then reckoned that Scientology was a fraud from beginning to end; a mind-numbing cult through and through. Since I had known Jason six years earlier and served as his Scientology counselor (auditor in Scientologese) for a short spell, and I believed that we had made some positive spiritual progress together, the Beghe interview hit me like a ton of bricks.

It was not so much what Jason said, it was how he said it that had the most impact on me. Here was a tortured soul. Here was a man madly striking back at some deep level of betrayal. Here was the once insouciant, irrepressible friend I had known reduced to a painful, cynical tirade of protest. From my twenty-seven years of involvement and conditioning in the church of Scientology – irrespective of my three years since on the outside looking in - my first reactive thought was to reject Jason and force myself not to empathize with him. But, try as I did, I could not ignore him.

Shortly after that Jason flew from California to our home in South Texas. We spent a week together. We swam in the Gulf of Mexico. We fished in Corpus Christi Bay. We drove by cotton fields in my pick-up truck with the windows down and the stereo blaring Springsteen full-blast while we hollered along. We sat on my deck late into each night watching the stars and passing ships and talking by the light of a chiminea (Mexican hearth). We talked of our expectations from Scientology, our hopes and our dreams and how those wishes had come to naught. I shared much of what I had learned as a student of life before and after Scientology and Jason exchanged pearls from his deep, rich similar past.

I offered Jason some auditing sessions (Scientology counseling). Jason agreed. We only did a couple of relatively short sessions. But, two things distinguished these sessions from the thousands of others I had participated in during my church of Scientology career. I had no other purpose than helping Jason in any way that I could as an auditor. Jason had unmitigated confidence that this purpose was present. As a result we both gained from the experience. I think that we both recognized that Scientology had initially served to strengthen and validate what was right about us and thus had increased our reach and feeling of well-being. But, at a certain point Scientology was utilized to try to rein us in, to control us and to make less of us.

I cannot say that we were able to undo twelve years of damage the church of Scientology had inflicted upon Jason or repair my twenty-seven years of conditioning on the inside. But, we both felt like we together had remedied a substantial amount of what was continuing to irk us about Scientology. A conclusion I drew from our meeting of minds was that Scientology could be likened to an enormous tool box. Its tools could be used to construct something or they could be used to destroy something. It all depended upon the intent of he who wields the tools. In either event, it was a powerful set of tools, which makes intent, or purpose, all the more important.

Over time Jason and I reckoned that during our week together we created a momentum that allowed us to eventually not only put our negative church experiences behind us but also to move on and up with our own spiritual journeys. Given that Jason never reached out again for more Scientology counseling, he came to a conclusion I could not have predicted. Jason told me that "problems created by Scientology need to be resolved with Scientology." That resonated as truth to me. It served to inform my decision to devote my attention to solving problems created by Scientology with Scientology. I decided that the manner in which he and I used certain Scientology tools was how they were intended to be used upon their creation. I recognized that there were probably more people in the world, by several multiples, who had experienced misuse of those tools and had left the increasingly corporatized churches of Scientology than there were of those who remained. I decided that I had a right, even a duty, to try to do what I could for that majority.

Since Jason's visit close to one hundred former members of the church of Scientology have sojourned to our home to resolve their Scientology experiences. The vast majority of them leave here still considering themselves Scientologists, and better ones than they were when they arrived. A smaller part of that majority continue on with their pursuit of higher levels of Scientology counseling and studies. A minority of those visitors consider that they have put Scientology behind them in a positive sense. That is to say, they are no longer struggling with and resisting memories of their pasts. They have reconciled them, and consider their Scientology experiences part of their own personal development – retaining positives and considering negatives as part of life's learning process.

These results are apparently upsetting and unacceptable to the church of Scientology (hereinafter referred to as Scientology Inc. or corporate Scientology so as to distinguish the organization from the philosophy and a growing movement of independent Scientologists). Since I have been practicing Scientology remedies on victims of corporate Scientology, extraordinary efforts have been made by the organization to crush me personally. I have been threatened by powerful Scientology lawyers on several occasions. My computers have been hacked. My phone records have been stolen. My cell phone gps device has been unlawfully used to track me. Airline reservation information has been hacked in order to terrorize my wife and me. My wife's co-workers and superiors have been intimidated in an effort to get my wife fired from her job. People I have counseled have been offered cash incentives to slander me. Thirty-five websites have been set up by Scientology Inc. to libel me and my wife. A number of covert agents were sent in attempting to infiltrate our home in the guise of former members who needed a hand. They even went so far as to lease a five bedroom home less than 200 yards from mine for several months. The house was manned by four to eight corporate Scientologists and private investigators at any given time. They harassed me and my wife on the doorstep of our home and virtually everywhere we traveled. I have been assured by Scientology Inc. agents that all I need to do in order for all of the harassment to cease is to stop practicing and talking about Scientology. Those agents, with cameras strapped to their heads, are captured on film shouting at me at the doorstep of my home on the cover of this book.

Fortunately, I was well-schooled in such tactics during my more than two decades at the top levels of corporate Scientology and so my wife and I have withstood the pressure with relatively little lasting damage done. However, I did recently recognize that, notwithstanding our demonstrated ability to survive the onslaught,

Scientology Inc. has been somewhat successful on one important count. They have distracted me from completing a very thorough history of the church of Scientology. That history will expose the how and why of corporate Scientology's metamorphosis into a sinister cult that uses Scientology to control and manipulate. I decided that in the event they are successful in their continuing attempts to prevent my complete exposure of the sordid operation's *why* – a rather gargantuan task - I had better get out the *what* and its remedy while I still have the chance. One need not have the *why* of the monster in order to identify and to remedy the very apparent *what* that the monster produces. In either event, Scientology Inc.'s why becomes somewhat clearer by simply describing what it has done and its reaction to the application of remedies to the harm it produces.

I have accumulated a wealth of information on how the practices of Scientology have been systematically manipulated to produce quite the opposite effect they were originally intended to create. The more I practice on the outside the more I learn about how that reversal of application has been institutionalized at every level of corporate Scientology. The more I learn, the more remedies – mostly, but not all, derived from Scientology itself – I witness work out well for people. Thankfully, I have found particularly workable Scientology Founder L. Ron Hubbard's advice that the larger and more complicated the situation, usually the lighter the touch and simpler the remedy works best. In fact, it seems that the most effective remedy is describing how a process, procedure or level of Scientology was supposed to be applied versus how it has come to be applied in Scientology Inc. A lot of relief can be had by connecting dots for someone who was never in a position to view the broader picture or to know what insanities and curve balls were implemented from the top of Scientology Inc. management.

The purpose of this book is to share the knowledge we have gained on how Scientology has been used to harm people and how that harm has been satisfactorily remedied. I hope that this learning can help other independent Scientology practitioners mend lives and assist with the spiritual advancement of former members of Scientology Inc. I expect that understanding how Scientology has been reversed in application and effect and the remedies for that might do a lot of good for former members, those who know former members, current members, those who interact with current members, for prospective members, and for those who are curious about the subject.

CHAPTER ONE

WHAT IS SCIENTOLOGY?

In order to understand what is wrong with Scientology, it will serve us well to establish what it is supposed to be. Try asking an active corporate Scientologist the simple question, what is Scientology? Chances are you will get back a hackneyed cliché, an inscrutable generality, or a tongue-tied, defensive response.

One of the problems with defining Scientology is that corporate members are encouraged to take all words of its creator L. Ron Hubbard literally. Since Hubbard pronounced so emphatically that it is strictly forbidden to pass on 'verbal technology,' (that is, explanations, definitions or technical data on Scientology not quoted directly from Hubbard's writings or lectures), and since Scientology Inc. takes his words and enforces them so literally, Scientologists find themselves afraid to discuss Scientology.

Let's examine 'verbal technology' a little more closely. Scientology is referred to as a technology within the church, because it sets itself apart from many other religions and philosophies by its myriad applications.

Scientologists pride themselves on applying a methodology that obtains certain results as opposed to simply believing in certain tenets.

Scientology has become not so much something to understand as it is something to apply. This is somewhat ironic, given the fact that Hubbard himself pronounced that the only way the subject of Scientology could be lost would be if its practitioners raised procedure into a position senior to understanding. Nonetheless, Scientologists for decades have been conditioned to never speak of Scientology without finding written or recorded words of Hubbard to quote from. And when it comes to interacting with the outside world, that muteness creates a lot of misunderstanding.

This state of affairs was exacerbated when, years after Hubbard's death, Scientology Inc. management created a several-hundred-page encyclopedic volume to answer the question, under the title *What Is Scientology?* Scientologists were encouraged to answer the oft-repeated question by disseminating this fifteen pound, very expensive book. Chock-full of self-praising platitudes, the book did more to create mystery and confusion than it did edification. The endeavor served little more than to help accelerate planetary deforestation.

Having been dubbed Scientology's heretic by the corporate group, I don't have any problem with attempting to answer the question without reference to anything but my first-hand experience. I will try to do in a few pages here what the church apparently failed to do in its six-hundred-plus-page glossy opus.

In 1950, L. Ron Hubbard published a book titled *Dianetics: The Modern Science of Mental Health*. Dianetics introduced the idea that the human mind could be viewed to contain two parts. First, the analytical mind, which we consciously use day in and day out to carry out rational, survival activity. Dianetics postulated that, absent interference, the analytical mind is an infallible computer.

Second is the reactive mind – the interference that fouls the analytical mind, making us irrational and reactive. The reactive mind stores all moments of partial or full unconsciousness, pain, and undesirable emotions and works on a stimulus-response basis. Stimuli in our environment can activate the reactive mind without our awareness and foul our analytical mind's otherwise perfect operation.

The reactive mind was presumably created in tooth-and-claw times, where constant stimulus-response reactivity was vital to survival. The reactive mind records all perceptions during moments of unconsciousness. The most destructive recordings are those containing words. That is because the reactive mind's stimulus-response character takes the words from a lowered-consciousness incident literally, and later feeds them back to a person – creating a post-hypnotic-suggestion effect on the individual. In this way the reactive mind overrides or influences the analytical mind, causing an individual to think and act irrationally.

Let's take a crude example. A child named Bill is knocked unconscious by a baseball bat in a Little League game. The force of the blow knocks out the function of his analytical mind and Bill collapses to the ground. While he lies injured, and unbeknownst to him analytically, his coach says loudly, "He's been knocked senseless."

Decades later, Bill, now a lawyer, goes to a ball game to take a break from a tough settlement negotiation he can't seem to bring to closure. He is upset. He has a few beers, which lowers his level of analytical awareness. Many of the same perceptions during his childhood head injury incident are present: the same late summer afternoon weather, the smell of freshly cut grass, the boisterous crowd chatter, the sense of two opposing forces competing, among others. These perceptions, in his lowered consciousness state 'key in' the reactive mind. The childhood incident, totally forgotten by Bill, is 'restimulated.' Bill begins to get a headache. That comes with the feeling and the idea that he has been "knocked senseless."

Bill goes to work the next day with a mild headache and the idea that he's been knocked senseless. When preparing for the final session of the settlement negotiation he left undone the day before, Bill wonders whether he has been acting senselessly. The pain in his head begins to subside as he complies with the idea the reactive mind is enforcing, that he has acted senselessly. Bill decides to drop a very strong and rational position he was on the verge of prevailing on in the negotiations because it seems "senseless." The negotiation is concluded.

Afterward, when Bill is called to account by his client for caving in on an issue of vast importance to the client, Bill rationalizes in a not-too-logical manner how it was "senseless" to pursue it. Thus, the reactive mind leads us toward negative or non-survival actions. It commands us below our level of awareness. The incidents dictating those actions are called 'engrams' (coined from the English word meaning 'trace on a cell').

The technology of Dianetics involves mentally returning to and recounting the moments of pain and unconsciousness in our lives so thoroughly as to nearly, in effect, relive them. The idea is that our resistance to fully viewing such incidents keeps them in place with sufficient force (e.g. stemming from the blow to the head many years before) to dictate later actions. When completely viewed, the emotional or mental 'charge,' or force, is relieved.

Each time we relieve such an incident, the memory of the occasion becomes available to the analytical mind. This in turn increases our rational or analytical memory and potential, as well as our outlook and abilities. When we relieve enough of said incidents, and have restored our hidden memories to our analytical mind, we achieve a state called 'Clear.' The term 'Clear' comes from the button on a calculator which clears a previous computation so that the machine can be used to address a new problem. And that is the goal of Dianetics: to clear the mind of the wrong answers that have been entered into it through painful past experiences.

The activity for relieving engrams is called 'auditing' (from the Latin root audire, to listen). A Dianetics or Scientology counselor is called an auditor. The person counseled is called the preclear (someone on the route to the state of Clear).

As Dianetics was more intensively practiced and the results were analyzed by Hubbard, matters became a bit more complicated. The further practitioners of Dianetics regressed down the mind's track of incidents (called the 'timetrack'), and the more awareness and perception was returned to the analytical side of the equation, the further back in time they could venture. Before long, Dianeticists were reporting incidents that occurred in previous lifetimes. This led to the conclusion that people are not simply genetic entities. The 'I' viewing and reporting on these incidents stored in the minds was something that transcended and outlived the genetic body, carrying on after death to start the cycle of birth-life-death all over again in a new body. The 'I' had many bodies over many lifetimes. It was resolved that this 'I' was the spirit.

So as not to confuse this discovery with terms and ideas from other subjects, Hubbard coined the term 'thetan' (taken from the Greek letter 'theta' which was used to symbolize 'thought' or 'spirit') to describe the spiritual essence and identity of each of us.

Dianetics proceeded from the fundamental premise that the lowest common denominator of life was the urge to survive. With the discovery and validation of the thetan, it was observed that this spiritual essence was not of the physical universe. The lowest common denominator could no longer be said to be 'survival.' After all, a thetan, not being inherently part of the create-survive-destroy cycle of the physical universe (a concept understood in spiritual circles since before the time of the Buddha, Siddhartha Gautama), could not help but survive; it was immortal.

An entirely new echelon of axioms evolved, beginning with the premise that the essential and common purpose of life was the creation of an effect. That led to the idea that the effects that life force could create were uncharted and presumably unlimited. A post-graduate study of Dianetics evolved.

Coined from the Greek scio, 'knowing,' and logos, 'study of,' Scientology was born. Hubbard, not presuming to have all the answers but ever curious about finding them, postulated that Scientology would be an unadulterated, unpoliticized, and uncorruptible search for ultimate truth, meaning, and immortality. Whereas Dianetics approached an individual from the perspective of removing negatives (engrams and the reactive mind), Scientology approached the individual more with a view toward rehabilitating and regaining inherent spiritual abilities.

Scientology evolved over the next two decades with Hubbard's continual experimentation with what was the most workable route to bring a thetan to the highest levels of truth, awareness and ability. Hubbard likened his creation of a gradient approach to enlightenment to building a bridge over a chasm, from a lower plane of existence to a higher one. He called the prescribed Scientology route of spiritual improvement 'the Bridge.' His life work was the building of a better bridge.

Hubbard looked for common points of difficulty along the Bridge and developed methods by which more people could overcome them. Part of that process was to undercut what he viewed as problems caused by societal trends. For instance, in the early 60s, Hubbard recognized degenerating educational standards among students newly attempting to study Scientology, and so he developed a course to teach a person how to learn.

Another example was the recognition in the late 60s, and again in the late 70s, of the prevalence, proliferation, and adverse spiritual effects of recreational and pharmaceutical drug use. He developed auditing programs, which he termed 'rundowns,' to address the mental and spiritual effects of drug use. In 1980 he undercut even further with a physical regimen for purifying the body of accumulated drugs and toxins.

Throughout his life Hubbard developed dozens of rundowns designed to undercut and speed progress up the Bridge. Many of those rundowns were so powerful that Scientologists elevated them to ends in their own right. That sometimes served to complicate a simple, concise description of what Scientology entails. The Bridge itself is the unchanging mainline spiritual route of Scientology. With that introduction, I present here the simplicity of the Scientology Bridge to spiritual freedom as I understand it.

Initially one addresses what is currently fixating one's attention and holding one back in life. There are a variety of short study courses available that can help one tackle such problems. Or one can partake in a short program of auditing called 'Life Repair,' specifically addressing, through auditing sessions, self-imposed barriers that are ruining the individual's life. If the individual has a history of extensive mind-altering drug intake, his or her next step would be what is called the Purification Rundown. This is a two-to-four week program of exercise, sauna, diet and supplements that cleanses residual drugs and toxins from the body.

Next an individual embarks upon the Scientology Grades (Six echelons of gradient spiritual enlightenment). The first Scientology grade is called 'ARC Straightwire.' 'ARC' refers to the components that define and describe the activity of life force ('theta') – that which an individual spiritual being (a thetan), and all living things, is made up of. A, R and C stand for Affinity, Reality and Communication. These three elements add up to Understanding. The idea is that in order to increase a being's understanding and capability, all one needs to do is raise either his Affinity, his Reality or his Communication with respect to any given person, subject or matter. If one raises any one of the three (A, R or C) the other two automatically rise proportionally and that translates to greater understanding.

'Straightwire' refers to the concept of stringing an imaginary wire from a thetan in present time to his memory banks, which of course are recordings of his past. ARC Straightwire consists of simple mental exercises designed to increase a person's ability to face his own past, incident by incident. This is accomplished by an auditor (Scientology counselor) running 'processes' with the person. A 'process' consists of a series of commands (directions to a preclear) to recall certain types of experiences. On ARC Straightwire one develops the ability to increase understanding of his own mind and of the environment.

Remarkably, virtually everyone who partakes of this grade at some point recognizes and originates to his auditor, in one way or another, that he or she will not get any worse as a spiritual being. That recognition signifies completion of ARC Straightwire.

A person who has completed ARC Straightwire then proceeds to Grade 0. Grade 0 addresses the subject of communication. The idea is that once a person can comfortably face his past and his present, he can now learn to communicate with them. The processes of Grade 0 bring about the understanding that virtually anything can be resolved with communication (mechanically, the interchange of particles or ideas between beings or between material objects or between a being and material objects). The processes increase one's willingness to communicate to, and receive and understand communication from, other people and his environment. Grade 0 processes are continued until such time as the preclear originates the ability and willingness to communicate with anyone on any subject.

Grade 1 is next. It deals with the subjects of help and problems. The first step of this grade involves processes that increase an individual's ability to comfortably face and change the physical environment (or matter, energy space and time – shortened to 'MEST' in Scientology). These are called Objective Processes. In this type of process, the auditor has the preclear observe and notice the physical environment and carry out changes in this physical environment.

An intensive (12 and ½ hour block of auditing) or two of Objective Processes usually is sufficient to assist an individual to a higher level of recognition of the difference between himself and the physical universe (MEST). A fair number of preclears have reported experiencing the phenomenon of 'exteriorization' during Objective Processing. 'Exteriorization' means that the thetan has separated out from the body, viewing it from a distance away while maintaining control of it. This usually comes as a significant spiritual revelation, the proof to many of their immortal spiritual nature.

When the Objective Processes are complete, the preclear runs a number of processes that help him to address the common experiences of failed attempts to help. These processes rehabilitate his own ability to help, and to receive help, by handling the upset of his past failures to help others, and others' past failures to help him.

The final leg of Grade 1 is problems processes. A problem is first defined as two opposing or conflicting intentions, purposes, or forces. Conceive of two gushing water hoses pointed at one another, and the resultant mass of turbulent, suspended water. Unresolved problems suspend mental mass and energy in time in this wise. Grade 1 has the preclear examine problems, past and present, from this perspective. The preclear continues to run processes on this grade until such time as she demonstrates a tremendous level of relief, and the ability to recognize the source of problems and, by doing so, routinely make them vanish with little to no effort.

Grade 2 addresses the source of hostilities and sufferings in life. This is often referred to as the 'confessional grade,' since its processes are almost entirely directed at the commission of transgressions, and the karmic results of such. In Scientology this is referred to as the Overt Act-Motivator Sequence. An 'overt act' is a destructive act committed by one against another. It is a transgression against what the thetan considers pro-survival conduct. When one commits an overt, he considers he will inevitably receive a motivator (a payback, or resultant counter effort). If one withholds (keeps hidden from others) one's overts and does not receive a motivator in due time, he will rationalize and imagine that the recipient of the original transgression first committed overts against him. This, in the person's mind, gives him a motivator for his own transgression, and seemingly justifies it. It also justifies or motivates the commission of more overts.

After committing an overt act, he will also withhold himself generally from life, and begin to punish himself (sub-consciously) for overts not actually "repaid" by motivators. Caught in this complex web, we accumulate many hostilities and sufferings in life. As one recalls and shares his own secret overt acts, as well as those others have committed against him, one begins to recognize the mechanism and free himself from it. Ultimately, one recognizes the Overt Act-Motivator sequence as the primary source of hostilities and sufferings.

Many Grade 2 completions report vast increases in memory, perceptions (particularly eyesight) and restored love for friends, family and humanity as a whole. In his numerous recorded lectures on this Grade, Hubbard contends that Grade 2 auditing proves over and over that thetans are basically good, because case after case recognizes that he punishes himself for his own transgressions before another can even learn of them, let alone begin to punish him for them. Further, once a person makes a clean breast of his life of shortcomings, he will, on his own determinism, tend to lead a more ethical, pro-survival existence. Rather than withhold his transgressions, a being tends to take responsibility for them of his own accord and move on in life, rather than pin himself back into the self-constructed hades of the Overt Act-Motivator Sequence.

Grade 3 deals with cleaning up upsets of one's past – which, after a thorough Grade 2, is often a simple, rather enjoyable task. Grade 3 processes free more and more attention to the present. A thetan's ability to tolerate and effectuate change is then tackled and increased. Having transcended the muck of the Overt Act-Motivator Sequence (essentially putting one in a position of causation in the matter of Karma), and learned to tolerate and effectuate changes in life, a being attains greater recognition of the power and seniority of the spirit over the physical universe. The end phenomenon (the event or realization that indicates a major Scientology action is complete) of Grade 3 is the freedom from upsets of the past, and the ability and willingness to face the future.

Listening to Hubbard's dozens of lectures on the development of Grade 4 is an enjoyable exercise. After fifteen years of research and development, during which he spoke in an engaged and insouciant manner, Hubbard's tone noticeably elevates over the course of explaining Grade 4 technology. It is his "Eureka!" moment in Scientology development. It is the level of the Bridge where the focus markedly shifts from removing disability to rehabilitating ability. The processes of Grade 4 result in a preclear moving out of fixed conditions into ability to do new things.

For most of the 60s and 70s, the Scientology Grades were prescribed to be applied after Dianetics auditing. Hubbard went back and forth on this question, and finally resolved that the Scientology Grades should be done before one embarks on Dianetics.

He reckoned this sequence for a couple of reasons. First, the Grades were discovered and developed as the resolution to the barriers to making a person Clear through Dianetics. They also happened to be, not surprisingly, the barriers to living life to its fullest. So, as one increased his abilities in life through the Grades, one also increased his spiritual horsepower and ability to confront and erase the significant mental energies and masses of the reactive mind (engrams). And so, the predecessor of Scientology, Dianetics, became the final step on the Scientology Bridge to the state of Clear.

Scientology processes – the Grades – are predominantly recall processes. That is, the preclear is asked to remember or bring to mind instances from his past and perceive them in the present. Recall processes are said to create stages of 'release.' A 'release' is a separation of the thetan from the reactive mind (or 'bank' in Scientologese). Dianetics processing is different. Dianetics involves running engrams (moments of pain and unconsciousness). 'Running an engram' means to return to and to thoroughly view the incident. Running engrams through Dianetics processing erases the anchor incidents (engrams) that might hold those Scientology realized abilities in an impermanent state.

Dianetics directly attacks the reactive mind engram bank and systematically relieves it of its mass and force upon a thetan. Usually, in the course of a few or several intensives of Dianetics auditing, a person has a realization and comes to terms with the relationship between the spirit, the mind and the physical universe. It is a profound revelation and brings about tremendous feelings of equanimity, compassion, and understanding.

Beyond that there are the Operating Thetan levels or OT Levels. Originally, Hubbard defined the idea of OT Levels as orientation of a cleared being to operating as a spiritual entity, separate and apart from the body. Much has been claimed by critics and denied by Scientology Inc. as to what the OT Levels involve. Excerpts from the OT Levels, outlining Hubbard's views about certain alleged events occurring long before the advent of human life as we know it have been mischaracterized as Scientology's 'creation myth.' Corporate Scientology's hysterical denials of the authenticity of the writings have served to solidify that misconception in the public mind.

While we will deal with the perversion of Scientology at the OT Levels in a later chapter, in this summary of what Scientology was intended to be and can be, it should be emphasized that every level of Scientology was designed to bring an individual up to higher levels of awareness and understanding. Every level was intended to build upon and bring further realization of the first ten Axioms of Scientology, written by L Ron Hubbard.

It is not different for the OT Levels, it is only a different paradigm and methodology toward a higher level of spiritual awareness. If anything, the first ten Axioms serve as Scientology's creation theory. They also happen to define what is addressed through all Scientology study and counseling, from bottom to top.

Axioms

Axiom One: Life is basically a static. (Definition: A life static has no mass, no motion, no wavelength, no location in space or in time. It has the ability to postulate and to perceive.) (Definition: In Scientology, the word 'postulate' means to cause a thinkingness or consideration. It is a specially applied word and is defined as causative thinkingness.)

Axiom Two: The static is capable of considerations, postulates and opinions.

Axiom Three: Space, energy, objects, form and time are the results of considerations made and/or agreed upon or not by the static, and are perceived solely because the static considers that it can perceive them.

Axiom Four: Space is a viewpoint of dimension. (Space is caused by looking out from a point. The only actuality of space is the agreed-upon consideration that one perceives through something and this we call space.)

Axiom Five: Energy consists of postulated particles in space. (One considers that energy exists and that he can perceive energy. One also considers that energy behaves according to certain agreed-upon laws. These assumptions and considerations are the totality of energy.)

Axiom Six: Objects consist of grouped particles and solids.

Axiom Seven: Time is basically a postulate that space and particles will persist. (The rate of their persistence is what we measure with clocks and the motion of heavenly bodies.)

Axiom Eight: The apparency of time is the change of position of particles in space.

Axiom Nine: Change is the primary manifestation of time.

Axiom Ten: The highest purpose in the universe is the creation of an effect.

CHAPTER TWO

BLACK DIANETICS

I spent more than twenty years of my life defending against the idea that Scientology practices could be harmful to a person. During the '80s and '90s, I directed the Scientology Inc. legal team in establishing a number of judicial precedents that recognized and protected Scientology practices as religious. I never considered during that entire time that the necessity for the First Amendment religious protections had anything to do with Scientology's potential for hurting people. It took three years of distance from Scientology and another four years of practicing Scientology with former church members, outside of and unaffiliated with the corporation, for me to finally recognize that Scientology, in the wrong hands, could wreak havoc on people.

Just before I left the organization for good in 2004, I had listened to a 1950s lecture by Hubbard in which he described a concept called 'Black Dianetics.' Hubbard said that charting the route to freeing people carried a liability. If one figures out and publishes how people are awakened from their usual hypnotic state by freeing them of the entrapment mechanisms of the human mind, a responsibility arises. If one finds the way out and makes it known, he also makes known the way to put a person into the morass. That is, for anyone twisted enough to care to reverse its processes for that purpose.

Hubbard described the idea in very crude terms. He asked listeners to examine the simplicity of how Dianetics and Scientology work. One makes sure a person is well fed, well rested and physically healthy before engaging in working with the mind and spirit. One creates a completely quiet and safe environment for the preclear. The auditor takes care never to invalidate nor evaluate for (tell a person what to think about himself, or about something being addressed) the preclear. This, in its simplicity, is what makes it possible for the preclear to examine his own mind and come to conclusions that increase his understanding and ability. It is what makes it possible for the person to wake up spiritually and become more self-determined, which is the purpose of Scientology auditing.

Hubbard then had the audience consider reversing those factors. Consider the effects of depriving a person of food and proper rest. Add to that a noisy and distracting environment. Then consider, instead of safely guiding the preclear to look to his own mind for answers, starting to supply the preclear with invalidation and evaluation – tell him he is no good, tell him he is basically bad. Hubbard said one could even reverse it more strongly. Starve the person and keep him from sleeping for days. Then administer physical beatings while shouting the commands, "You are bad" and "You are no good." Hubbard noted that it was fairly easy to see that if kept up for long the precise opposite of the product of a Dianetics or Scientology auditing session would be produced. Instead of the person walking out brighter, more intelligent and self-determined, the person would crawl out thinking he was a beaten, good-for-nothing dog.

The first point that Hubbard was trying to get across was that the trust an auditor is granted by a preclear is sacred. It carries a responsibility to be sure that one does Dianetics and Scientology by the book, because to not have those factors present that make freeing an individual possible is tantamount to doing the opposite, to one degree or another.

The second point he made was that the potential for reversing the process highlights the need to create a positive ethic in Dianetics and Scientology. In other words, auditors need to demonstrate a high level of ethics before being entrusted with the spiritual fate of a preclear.

I could not appreciate the full implications of that lecture while listening at that time. I had just escaped the Scientology international headquarters near Hemet, California. I had returned temporarily to Scientology's spiritual retreat in Clearwater, Florida, in an effort to resolve matters with my then wife – who was, like me, a lifetime Scientology Inc. staff member. My attention was riveted to my recent experiences at Scientology's headquarters where its supreme leader David Miscavige was subjecting members of international management to virtually everything Hubbard noted as being detrimental to their mental and spiritual health. Miscavige had recently locked up 80-some managers at the Hemet headquarters, including me. They were imprisoned. They were deprived of food. They were deprived of sleep. They were beaten, hazed and humiliated, all while Miscavige rained insults upon them as to their lack of competence, ethics, courage, and standing as human beings. I had, in fact, decided to escape the moment I recognized that Miscavige had accomplished that end product with a number of members of management, whom he had effectively subjected to this treatment for months. I withstood these conditions for four days before reckoning that Miscavige wanted to put me in the same broken condition he had already apparently accomplished with others.

Listening to the Black Dianetics lecture was a turning point for me. I demanded to meet with Miscavige to discuss how he was treating dozens of top Scientology managers precisely in the manner Hubbard noted an evil person would treat them, if his purpose was to depower them, entrap them, and destroy them mentally and spiritually. Miscavige, through an intermediary, agreed to meet me on my objections to Black Dianetics being practiced at the highest levels of Scientology management. However, Miscavige managed to have emergencies conveniently arise that caused several cancellations. After months, it became clear to me that the agreed-upon meeting would never materialize. Only then did I leave Corporate Scientology for good.

After three years of decompression from my 27-year experience within Scientology Inc. I began meeting with old Scientologist friends again. The more I learned of their experiences and the more I learned from counseling former members, the more I recognized how Black Dianetics had become an ever-expanding practice within Miscavige's cult. It wasn't just Miscavige's evil intentions being acted out upon a single group of people. It had trickled down the entire international Scientology network of groups and infected virtually every service they offered.

The potential for such abuse of Scientology for ulterior motives is made clear in Hubbard's own description of what mechanically occurs between an auditor and a preclear in an auditing session:

The auditor and pre-clear are a group. To function well a group must be cleared. The clearing of a group is not difficult. It requires but little time. The relationship of the auditor and pre-clear is not parity. The auditor lends himself to the group as the control center of the group until the pre-clear's sub-control center is established under his own control center's command. The role of the auditor ceases at that moment. The auditor necessarily owns the pre-clear. He owns the pre-clear on a lessening basis until the pre-clear owns himself. If the auditor wishes to successfully own, to the end of NOT owning, the pre-clear, he must not use the pre-clear to the service of the auditor, for this establishes and confirms the ownership and inhibits the pre-clear from owning himself.

Increasingly within corporate Scientology, the organizations take the initially established control the auditor necessarily establishes, and use it to direct the preclear to the service of the organizations. I searched out more of Hubbard's 1950s warnings about the danger of the reversal of Dianetics and Scientology processes. I found out that Hubbard was emphatic, even dramatic, about the concern. Here is a passage from a lecture on Black Dianetics delivered in December, 1952:

Contained in the knowable, workable portions before your eyes there are methods of controlling human beings and thetans which have never before been dreamed of in this universe. Control mechanisms of such awesome and solid proportions that if the remedies were not so much easier to apply, one would be appalled at the dangerousness to beingness that exists in Scientology.

Hubbard contended in that same lecture that he developed Scientology with this concern in mind, and so built in remedies for such possible misuse: *"Fortunately, it was intelligently invented, and I say that without any possible bow; I say that because part of its logic was: the remedy should exist before the bullet."*

Indeed, a great deal of future development in Scientology through the '60s and '70s was along the line of remedies for misapplications of Scientology. However, after Hubbard's 1986 death, the remedies for misuse of Scientology began to be used increasingly to enforce the misuses. The technology of restoring self-determinism to individuals was increasingly being twisted and used to create the opposite – tractable and compliant cult members.

Ironically, over the ensuing three decades Hubbard's own strict organizational policies enforcing an unquestioning loyalty to the authorized central organization of the church of Scientology wound up being used as weapons to protect and forward the institutionalized practice of Black Dianetics. Those very policies crippled what he once considered the most important, effective prophylactic against widespread implementation of Black Dianetics. The following 1952 warning by Hubbard apparently turned out to be prophecy:

So anybody that knows the remedy of this subject, anybody that knows these techniques, is himself actually under a certain responsibility — that's to make sure that he doesn't remain a sole proprietor. That's all it takes, just don't remain a sole proprietor. Don't ever think that a monopoly of this subject is a safe thing to have. It's not safe. It's not safe for Man; it's not safe for this universe. This universe has long been looking for new ways to make slaves. Well, we've got some new ways to make slaves here. Let's see that none are made.

Sixty years later, the very central organization Hubbard created has become that monopoly, making an institutional practice of creating slaves through Black Dianetics. For the past 50 years, many have attempted to avert Hubbard's prediction by breaking the monopoly. Most of those efforts have been smashed through the sophisticated and ugly intelligence, propaganda and litigation machine that Scientology Inc. has become.

For the past three years, I have been working with a growing network of independent Scientologists to apply Hubbard's ultimate remedy. That is, for the first time in the 60-plus-year history of the subject we are breaking the monopoly by protecting and proliferating the use of Scientology independently. Only in this independent field is Scientology being applied as originally intended, for the sole purpose of increasing the self-determinism, the spiritual awareness and abilities of those it is applied to.

Much has been learned about how to restore these qualities to former Scientology Inc. members. The first and most important step in any recovery is correctly identifying the problem. In the following chapters we will identify the precise manner in which Black Dianetics has been injected into the Scientology Inc. lineup at every level.

CHAPTER THREE

TRAINING

The best place to begin unraveling the reversal of the subject of Scientology is with auditor training. After all, curve balls thrown into the training lineup effect virtually every session delivered by auditors produced by that training. As noted in the last chapter, my introduction to the subject of Black Dianetics began with Hubbard using a crude example. He started with the fundamental elements of what makes auditing work – the safe environment, the auditor there to help the preclear, and the auditor listening without interrupting, invalidating or evaluating. In short, the creation of an environment where a preclear can easily look for answers, share them and come to new realizations.

The foundation of auditing technology is communication. This is in keeping with the central idea in Scientology that Understanding is composed of Affinity, Reality and Communication. By increasing Communication, Affinity and Reality automatically increase and we experience greater Understanding. A myriad of salutary ripple effects are imaginable, stemming from application of this simple formula. Accordingly, the first training course for an auditor treats the subject of communication.

Communication is inextricably connected with Affinity and Reality in bringing about Understanding (the purpose of Scientology auditing). And thus a thoroughgoing understanding of and adherence to the idea of maintaining and increasing the ARC triangle is a constant throughout an auditor trainee's communication training.

To master ARC through communication, an auditor engages in a course of Training Routines (TRs). The TRs first train the auditor to sit comfortably and face a preclear; do nothing but comfortably face the preclear for a substantial period of time. Hubbard noted that a blink, a blush, a twitch, a fidget, a re-adjusting oneself in one's seat, all can serve to distract a preclear – or worse. Discomfort demonstrated by an auditor can imply more than a lack of auditor comfort, to a preclear. Such seemingly innocent body movements or changes could make the preclear think that the auditor is bored with what the preclear is saying, or even disapproves of what the preclear is saying. And that would of course tend to invalidate or evaluate for the preclear. Thus, the first TRs involve training an auditor to comfortably sit for hours with no body reactions whatsoever.

These drills are both challenging, rewarding, and can have a powerful spiritual effect on a trainee. In fact, if high standards are maintained by a TRs supervisor, profound changes occur with the auditor. The trainee learns that the only way to survive the mental and physical pressures that his own mind and body inevitably impose on him is to simply be there and face them. He learns that resisting or attempting to suppress the discomfort can exacerbate it. But when the auditor does nothing more than practice the simplicity of just being there and perceiving, the discomforts dissolve. In this way the initial TRs act like the highest and purest form of spiritual meditation. In well-supervised TRs courses many students have reported exteriorizing from their bodies.

Once this stable foundation is laid, the gradient is upped by having a mock preclear, or coach, 'bullbait' the auditor trainee. Bullbaiting is harassing or distracting the trainee in any way the coach can: insulting him, entertaining him to laughter, attempting to embarrass him, etc. The trainee develops the ability to be there comfortably despite every provocation to make him react. Besides being a lot of fun, bullbaiting results in an even more stable, comfortable state of being for the auditor trainee.

TRs then graduate into drilling all parts of a cycle of communication. The auditor learns to deliver his own communication so that it is natural, clear, understandable and pleasant to receive. He then drills to be able to fully duplicate and understand that which a preclear communicates to him, and to acknowledge it well, so that the preclear knows the auditor fully got what was said.

Next comes drilling on giving a repetitive command. Many Scientology processes require the same direction or question be delivered over and over until the preclear has examined the subject from multiple points of view, and come to a cognition (a new realization about life). An untrained auditor can make such processes have the reverse effect, by sounding like a robotic repeating machine. This level of the TRs teaches an auditor to deliver the same command repetitively, each time in its own new unit of time, freshly – as if each time were the first time the question or direction had occurred to him. This skill is integral in maintaining interest.

Once the repetitive question is mastered, the auditor drills all elements of an auditing session, with the coach acting as a real preclear, manifesting all the things a preclear might in an actual session – from falling asleep, to failing to answer the question, to distracting the auditor, to not understanding the question or command, to suddenly originating something important to him, but totally off the subject of the session.

The one constant that must be nurtured through all TRs training is the maintenance of a high level of ARC – evident Affinity, Reality and Communication between auditor and preclear. The end product of the TRs is a person who can naturally, easily run an auditing session while maintaining a beingness (personality and bearing) that a preclear finds is almost irresistible to comfortably open up to.

Now, here is the Scientology Inc. Black Dianetics rub. Since approximately 1995, David Miscavige has commandeered and micro-managed the training of auditors. He has done so by making his organization, the Religious Technology Center (RTC), the central and only final authority for each and every auditor trainee's quality of TRs. Auditor trainees must submit video recordings of themselves performing TRs for RTC representatives to review. Those representatives in turn are directly trained by Miscavige to assume and enforce the beingness of Miscavige himself. The beingness of Miscavige, by his own proud proclamation, is that of ruthless, hard, chrome steel.

What has ensued since Miscavige's takeover of all TRs training is an eternal struggle between the imposed cruel, steely beingness of the cult leader, and the purpose and end product of the TRs: the mastering of communication with affinity and reality so as to bring about understanding. The two sides of the struggle are polar opposites.

And so, ultimately, Scientology Inc.-trained auditors wind up falling somewhere in the spectrum between a selfless, helping, friendly counselor and a cold, chrome, ruthless enforcer. To Scientology purists there are no in-betweens. Pure affinity, reality, and communication so as to bring about understanding is infected with the virus of a synthetic personality imposing its will upon the preclear. The auditor is either present and doing nothing but being there for the preclear, seamlessly and, in a way, invisibly applying the processes of Scientology, or he is doing something else. The latter cannot help but be a distraction or an impediment. After all, the entire purpose of the TRs is to produce an auditor who can eliminate additives to pure A, R and C which might distract or impede a preclear's ability to divine the truth. This is a fundamental flaw of corporate Scientology, as it affects every auditing session at every level of the Scientology Bridge.

L. Ron Hubbard noted that only an auditor with impeccable TRs (communication skills) could master the art of metering. Metering refers to the operation of the Hubbard electro-psychometer, or e-meter. Metering is the next level of Scientology auditor training.

The e-meter is a simple device. Its primary internal component is a Wheatstone bridge, a device that measures the resistance to a flow of electricity through a medium or circuit. Thoughts that persist (engrams and those thoughts carrying emotional or mental stress) contain a minute, yet impressionable and detectable electric charge. Charged thoughts are detectable by creating a very light electric circuit through the body (using less voltage than that of a flashlight battery). This circuit is created when a preclear holds a simple electrode, much like a metal can, in each hand; the electrodes are connected to the meter.

When there is a mental, emotional or spiritual charge connected with a subject touched upon in a session, it creates a movement of a needle on the e-meter, which the auditor can see. Such a movement is called a 'read.' If the meter reads when a new subject is introduced by the auditor, the auditor knows that there is charge connected to that subject, with that particular preclear. The read tells the auditor to go ahead and run the appropriate Scientology process. If the meter does not read, or register, when a subject is introduced, it means the subject carries no impact, and thus there is no sense in taking it up with that particular preclear.

The magic of the meter is that it reads just below the preclear's level of awareness. If the preclear were fully aware of the underlying aspects of what was bothering him, it wouldn't bother him. In order for something to be a problem or source of upset to a preclear, there must be things about it that he is not completely aware of, or about which he is mistaken. By uncovering and thoroughly examining troublesome areas lying just below his current level of awareness, the preclear can understand them completely, and their adverse effects vanish. As a result, his overall awareness and spiritual well-being also increase.

As one can imagine, the introduction of such a contraption into the equation of an auditing session might be rather distracting or intimidating, from the preclear's perspective. If you think that might be the case, you are not alone. L. Ron Hubbard was acutely aware of this very possibility. That is why he put even more emphasis on TRs, and required that an auditor train with a meter to a point where he was so confident and natural in handling it that the preclear does not even notice its presence in an auditing session. This is not an easy accomplishment, but it is an achievable one. A good auditor masters the operation of the meter to the point where he is so smooth with it that its presence does not detract in the slightest from the foundation of the session: the communication cycle between the preclear and auditor.

Here is where Black Dianetics has been introduced into e-meter training. The Miscavige regime has promoted the e-meter as some all-knowing, all-powerful, high-tech artifact worthy of fear and worship. It has raised the technology of metering to some hallowed plane, far above the art and science of the true active agent in spiritual healing, the communication formula.

Miscavige has personally introduced technical changes to the simple Wheatstone bridge, with great fanfare. In fact, the technical adjustments Miscavige has introduced have, if anything, detracted from the e-meter's basic effectiveness. Nonetheless, he has promoted such "improvements" to all Scientologists with such hoopla that they actually believe his physical adjustments have fundamentally improved the art and science of Scientology. So supposedly important and basic are these "new, improved" e-meter models that on at least two occasions Miscavige has made it Scientology Inc. policy that all Scientologists must trash their existing meters and purchase not one, but two, of his "new, improved" editions. When each Scientologist has to scrape together $2,500 to $5,000 a meter for these "breakthroughs," they can't help but rationalize that the new meters must be revolutionary and all-important. The degree to which they rationalize in this way is the degree they devalue what actually brings about improvement with a preclear: the auditing cycle and formula of communication.

Miscavige's brand of auditor training sears that "importance" into the minds of auditors with an atomic branding iron. As with the TRs, Miscavige has required that all e-meter training students receive their final passes – and thus certificates – from his own RTC representatives. Since 1995, those RTC representatives have, for the most part, held a distinction that no great auditor can claim. That is, most of David Miscavige's RTC representatives have not delivered substantial amounts of Scientology auditing. They have used e-meters to interrogate people, they have used e-meters to intimidate people, they have used e-meters for all manner of aggressive purposes. But they have never made a living as professional auditors. Few have ever even held the position of auditor in a Scientology organization, and so they are uniquely unqualified to pass judgment on the standards of e-meter operation. In this respect, they have been molded in the image of their creator.

David Miscavige who has not delivered an auditing session himself since early '70s has issued so many arbitrary dictates as to what constitutes a meter read, and then altered and canceled and reinstated those arbitraries so many times, that Scientology Inc. auditors now have their attention glued to the e-meter. Even more destructively, Miscavige had the temerity to cancel L. Ron Hubbard's description of what constitutes a floating needle. A floating needle (or F/N) is an e-meter needle phenomenon that indicates the preclear has achieved a state of release from the reactive mind, and thus that the process or session should be smoothly ended. The needle lazily glides back and forth across the meter dial. Hubbard has described it as a 'free' needle – as if suddenly the needle detaches from some sort of invisible restraint, and virtually floats across the dial. A floating needle is such a distinct, easily-recognizable phenomenon that Hubbard noted, "You'll know one when you see one. They're really pretty startling. The needle just idles around and yawns at your questions on the subject."

Miscavige arbitrarily dictated that a floating needle, as defined by Hubbard, was not a floating needle, and was not to be treated as a floating needle until the needle swung, stopped, swung back in the other direction, and then did so once again. This was called the "three-swing" floating needle. Auditors since 1995 have been trained, upon threat of such penalties as sleep deprivation and heavy manual labor assignments, not to indicate a needle is floating until they have carefully counted three separate sweeps of the needle in its free state. That injunction has served to cancel a primary Hubbard axiom on the subject of metering. A student of metering is emphatically warned by Hubbard of the dangers of "waiting for the meter to play Dixie." By this is meant hesitating even for a fraction of a second to recognize and appropriately react to any significant meter needle reaction.

When an auditor hesitates in a session and fixes his attention on the meter, the preclear's attention also goes to the meter. And thenceforth the meter is no longer reading on the preclear and his or her mind, it is reading on the preclear's thoughts and considerations about the meter and the auditor's attention on the meter. If an auditor is unfortunate enough to create this state of affairs, he experiences an auditing session ruined.

The havoc that the "three-swing" floating needle arbitrary has wreaked upon the practice of Scientology is hard to describe. Perhaps the best analogy would be with reference to the TRs and the injunction against evaluating for or invalidating the preclear. Assume there is no meter present, and a Scientology process is being run. The preclear becomes bright and cheery, and announces, "You know, I finally figured out why I have problems with my mother; I keep creating them. Gee, I can't wait to clear this up with Mom and catch up on the years we've been out of communication." By nervously staring at the meter in response the auditor is effectively responding: "Hold on a minute, let me evaluate what you just said and determine whether that realization is worthy of ending this process."

For an auditor to do this would be strictly prohibited evaluation and invalidation, and would kill that preclear's sense of accomplishment and satisfaction. And that is precisely what happens when an auditor waits for an e-meter to play Dixie. The second that occurs, the mental state that caused the needle to float disappears, to be replaced by a disappointed, worried state that will cause the needle to stick again. If this chain of events is repeated, before long, auditing sessions degenerate into complicated games – the preclear by necessity dreaming up all manner of shifts to make the needle float, in order to complete the session. Many subjected to this style of metering have reported resorting to purposely thinking unrelated pleasant thoughts, in an effort to make the needle float.

As a result of Miscavige's arbitrary dictates, an e-metering course that should be completed in two to three weeks of full-time training – as was routinely done during Hubbard's life – now routinely takes many months or even years to navigate. By the time a Miscavige corporate Scientology student completes e-meter training, he or she has in many respects become the meter: his communication "skills" are as mechanical as the device he has been brainwashed to alternately fear and worship.

The net result of Miscavige's foundational TRs and metering training is the destruction of the original idea of a Scientology auditing session. When a preclear is engaging in a Scientology auditing session effectively, he is said to be 'in-session.' 'In-session' was defined by Hubbard very simply as "interested in own case (mind and its problems) and willing to talk to the auditor." Nothing could reverse that state of affairs more thoroughly than a hard, chrome steel countenance, arrogantly lording it over the preclear behind an all-powerful, mind-altering machine. Thus, Miscavige has ingrained Black Dianetics most effectively and thoroughly through his commandeering and perversion of Scientology auditor training.

The remedies for Miscavige's Black Dianetics training are simple. People approaching auditor training for the purpose of attaining skills with which to help another individual clear himself of the mental, emotional and spiritual travails of life find Hubbard's materials on the TRs and metering rather clear and straightforward. One doesn't need to find a genius to help unravel the mysteries of how it is really done. A dozen or so Hubbard bulletins, a couple of lectures on TRs, the Hubbard books *E-meter Essentials*, *Understanding the E-meter*, and *Book of E-meter Drills*, and the handful of Hubbard bulletins and lectures on the art and science of metering are all it takes.

Although Miscavige has spent decades trying to convince Scientologists that these materials are confusing, contradictory, and impossible to understand, any person of average intelligence, and with the purpose to help others, will find them rather simple to grasp and apply effectively.

CHAPTER FOUR

RUDIMENTS

David Miscavige often presents himself to Scientologists as the "finder of lost tech." He routinely digs up some decades-old, out-of-context remarks from L. Ron Hubbard and foists them off as the lost key to the kingdom, explaining why Scientology didn't work as well with folks as it should have. He stages four to six internationally-broadcast events per year, where he re-plays this sophistry show against a backdrop of blaring music and sound effects, accentuated by glitzy, overwhelming visuals. Before Scientologists can regain their senses from the extravaganzas, they are bullied into buying expensive new packages of materials or services based on Miscavige's "discoveries."

Through this dazzling con, corporate Scientology ventures further and further from the solid foundation that makes the auditing process actually work. In Las Vegas spectacle fashion, in 1996 Miscavige unveiled his ultimate solution to the "inability" of people to comprehend what he implied was the incomprehensible: the L. Ron Hubbard materials on the training of auditors. Miscavige appeared on stage with hundreds of manuals that he had directed be created to explain, clarify and direct one in how to apply Hubbard's writings on auditor training. In all of that vast material, hardly a word could be spared on the subject of what an auditor must first do in order to get a preclear in session to begin with.

Corporate Scientology has become quite adept at taking a preclear's money and routing him into an auditing room with an auditor. It is very accomplished at these two steps. But that does not constitute Hubbard's definition of a preclear being 'in session': *interested in own case and willing to talk to the auditor.*

To create the condition of 'in session' for a preclear requires that the auditor first address himself. He must adjust his own attitude and intentions appropriately. In his 1951 book, *Advanced Procedure and Axioms*, Hubbard highlighted this fact:

THE FIRST ACT of the auditor concerns himself. He assesses the task rather than the pre-clear and assesses the matter within himself. He establishes whether or not he desires the pre-clear to become established under the pre-clear's own center of control. To do this the auditor may find it necessary to straight-wire himself for the removal of any reason why he does not want this pre-clear to be owned by the pre-clear. He then postulates to himself what he wants to happen with this pre-clear and postulates as well that he can do this task with this pre-clear. He must feel these postulates solidly. If he cannot he must discover why he cannot. Thus the first session's first minutes with the pre-clear are concerned with the auditor himself. He should take time out from the pre-clear until he himself is established in his task and then readdress the pre-clear.

The auditor must first determine for himself that he wants to increase the self-determinism of the preclear. He must wholeheartedly embrace the idea that whatever processes he applies, he applies them for the purpose of increasing the preclear's ownership of herself. This injunction would take on far more importance after a several-year training regimen in corporate Scientology, aimed at fixating an auditor trainee on being in total control. The chrome, cold steel countenance of the Miscavige auditor comes into session with quite a different set of purposes than what Hubbard prescribed.

Second only to the first purpose of controlling and owning the preclear, the Scientology Inc. auditor's next purpose is to stay out of trouble. The way to stay out of trouble is to ensure one's preclears become increasingly loyal to Scientology Inc. leadership. The corporate Scientology auditor is drilled within an inch of his life never to allow a preclear through who harbors the slightest doubt or critical attitude about Miscavige and his measures. He learns that if a preclear he audits is later found to demonstrate or confess the slightest glimmer of negativity toward Miscavige and his programs, that auditor can be severely punished.

The vehicle through which a corporate Scientology auditor learns to accomplish that sort of loyalty check is called the 'rudiments.' The term was borrowed from the English, rudiments: fundamental facts or principles. In Scientology, it means those fundamentals that must be present or 'in' for an auditing session to proceed. Most importantly, what is required to be 'in' is the preclear's attention. Those factors in his current life that might drag his attention out of session would make the preclear 'out-rudiments' (short-handed to 'out ruds' in Scientologese).

The tools to put rudiments 'in' in Scientology consist of three questions that an auditor checks at session start, if the needle of the e-meter is not floating (indicating a distraction-free, desirable frame of mind). The questions were intended to detect that small handful of possible mental distractions that could prevent a preclear from being thoroughly interested in his own case and willing to talk to the auditor.

The three questions are:

- Do you have an ARC break? (an upset or, technically, a recent sundering in affinity, reality, or communication with some person or some issue in one's environment)

- Do you have a present time problem? (i.e., is there some uncared-for task or un-confronted confusion that might yank your attention out of session?)

- Has a withhold been missed? (i.e., is your attention caught up, maybe even just on a subconscious level, with having a transgression of yours revealed?)

Now, most preclears have paid handsomely for their auditing and they are happy to get the show on the road when they arrive to the auditing room. And with that happiness comes, quite routinely, a floating needle. But, as we noted in the last chapter on training, Scientology Inc. auditors are trained to disregard floating needles until they have danced for several moments: the "three-swing floating needle."

Nine times out of ten, when the auditor fixates on counting the swings, the preclear's attention goes to the auditor, an upset ensues and the floating needle instantly dies. Had the auditor said, "Your needle is floating. The first process we are going to run is…," the needle would have kept on floating until the preclear's attention was focused on the first process in the then-begun body of the auditing session. But that doesn't happen in corporate Scientology. Instead, the good-soldier, Scientology Inc. auditor waits for the floating needle to die while counting its swings, then starts rattling off the rudiments questions.

Because the auditor missed the initial floating needle, he drove the preclear's rudiments out, and now a vicious cycle ensues. The problem is exacerbated by Scientology Inc. auditors' pre-occupation with using the rudiments to assure his preclears remain loyal to Miscavige. Hubbard envisaged the type of auditor Miscavige has created: one who is obsessed with the rudiments of the preclear – obsessed with prying into the details of his present life and circumstances. Hubbard even noted that fixation on rudiments would drive rudiments further out, in a 1961 lecture appropriately titled Basics of Auditing:

Now, let's take the first object lesson here: The auditor sits down in the auditing chair; the PC (preclear) sits down in the PC's chair. What is the contract? What is the understood contract as of that instant? That understood contract is a very simple contract: The PC sat down to be audited. What does the PC understand by 'being audited?' He basically understands it as getting on toward Clear. What he means "toward Clear," we're not sure a lot of the time, but even that: he senses it is there, he senses he's got a direction to go, he senses that he can arrive at a certain destination, and he's there to get that done. Now, he's not there to have ARC breaks run, present time problems handled; he's not there to straighten out the auditing room; he's not there to have any of these things done at all that we call rudiments. He is there to get audited toward Clear. Well, the first observation we can make: that rudiments go out to the degree that auditing doesn't get done. That's a direct ratio. Rudiments go out to the degree that auditing does not get done.

Hubbard goes on to describe a vicious circle the auditor creates. The continual auditor fixation on present-time rudiments becomes the out rudiment – in this case, the 'present time problem' of the preclear. Hubbard notes that out of respect for the auditor, the preclear won't complain and will assign another reason for the e-meter reads the auditor is addressing, and begin to invent problems. Before long, the entire activity of auditing is a created mind game which gets the preclear nowhere but further introverted.

Hubbard also noted in several other lectures on auditing that the preclear's attention concentrates where the auditor directs it. In fact, the auditor is trained into the ability to direct the preclear's attention. When the auditor repeatedly drives the attention of the preclear onto rudiments, the preclear's attention goes further and further onto the subject of rudiments. The end result is an insecure person, fixated on the present upsets and problems of life. In short, the polar opposite of what Scientology intends to and is capable of producing.

The remedy for preclears who've been subjected to such treatment is to patch up upsets which corporate Scientology auditors have created. Then do like Hubbard said in the first place and honor the unwritten contract you as an auditor entered into with the preclear. The auditor's side of the bargain is to audit the preclear towards Clear.

CHAPTER FIVE

OBJECTIVES

Objective Processes in Scientology consist of precise steps directed at getting a preclear into communication with his physical (objective) environment, mostly through sight and tactile perception. Objectives increase one's objective certainty as well as give him a greater appreciation for his own spiritual identity, separate and apart from the mind and body. A lot of people have wonderful experiences on their Objective Processes. Even though it is not required or even expected to occur, a great many of them have reported exteriorizing from their heads and viewing their own body and the room from above, in the course of doing Objectives. Conversely, during the running of any given Objective Process (before it is complete), all manner of physical and mental pain can manifest. A good Objectives auditor learns that the three oldest rules of auditing are particularly applicable when pain and discomfort do materialize:

- A. What turns it (the discomfort) on will turn it off.

- B. The way out is the way through.
- C. Get the preclear through it.

Some people have had miserable experiences with Objective Processes. They have reported being led to the mental and physical pain stage, but never making it through. My own experience has been that the majority of negative experiences were occasioned by an auditor either failing to apply the three oldest rules (A, B, and C above) and ending off sessions while the preclear was still experiencing physical or mental heaviness, or continuing to grind through processes after the preclear had experienced their intended end phenomena.

The processes are considered to be complete when the preclear has a major recognition that it is he, the thetan, who is in charge of himself as an entity. To one degree or another, he wakes up to the fact that it is he, the thetan, who runs the mind and body. The expected end phenomena of Objective Processes are clearly stated by Hubbard as follows:

- They remedy havingness (repair, restore or increase the ability to tolerate, reach and permeate one's physical environment)
- They locate the person in his or her environment.
- They establish direct communication with the auditor.
- And last but not least, they bring a person to present time.

The basic activity of Objectives is the auditor commanding the preclear to carry out mundane physical tasks. The preclear's reactive mind usually puts up resistance to such control, and the preclear dramatizes that resistance back at the auditor. The auditor persists, controlling the preclear and his body (never dropping his affinity, reality, and communication) until such time as the preclear realizes that the body and mind can be controlled, and starts doing so himself. At that point, simple as it may seem, the preclear routinely has a huge leap in self-determinism. Or, to paraphrase an earlier Hubbard quote in this book, the auditor rehabilitates the preclear as center of control of his own body and mind, and turns that control center over to the preclear for good.

It is vital that Objective Processing end there. If it does not, what happens? The auditor overrides the self-determinism of the preclear. Further, the desired self-determinism realization and rehabilitation are bypassed and replaced by a new decision by the preclear – something along the lines of, "Better that I just forfeit control and let the auditor and Case Supervisor decide when to stop." The longer self-determinism is forfeited, the more overwhelmed the preclear becomes. And the more willing he becomes to be other-determined. The continued mundane compliance drill becomes a sort of perverse conditioning in how to tolerate and comply with senseless orders.

The preclear's new other-determinism decision is locked in place and buried by mental masses. This phenomenon is called 'overrun' (something run too long) and the results are described by Hubbard:

Overrun occurs when the thetan considers that something has gone on too long or happened too often. When the person begins to feel this way about something, he begins to protest it and try to stop it. This tends to make things more solid and builds up mass in the mind.

Once a person has achieved the end phenomena of Objective Processes, it is expected that he takes what he learns with him. In other words, he obtains some understanding that in order to get one's attention unfixed from the past, and thus free oneself from the mental forces and masses connected with the past, all one need do is establish communication with his environment and contact present time. It is an ability-attained condition. It is not a five-minutes-of-relief affair that need be repeated.

This fact compounds the felonies perpetrated by Scientology Inc.'s misuse of objectives.

In the face of all this David Miscavige has somehow managed to institute, throughout corporate Scientology, the following policies:

• Objectives Processes are to be done for many, many intensives (12½ hour blocks of auditing), irrespective of attainment of the end phenomena of Objectives.
• Objectives Processes are to be run on Clears and OTs (those Clears who have embarked on higher levels of Scientology) who have spent decades and hundreds of thousands of dollars progressing up the Bridge since completing Objectives the first time.

Miscavige even had the Senior technical expert of one of the highest Scientology organizations (the late Richard Reiss) issue a directive that Objectives were to be run on everyone, for periods up to and exceeding 120 hours. Even the 120 hours was only a gradient, public-relations approach, geared to the public at large. Miscavige himself briefed high-level Scientologists in an annual "summit" that he wanted people put through far more than 120 hours of Objectives. These are his own words with respect to enforcement of Objective Processing:

And what do I want him to do? 200, 300, 400 – you want to do 600 hours? Go for it, bud. Go and go and go and go and go and go and go.

In the light of the purpose of Objective Processes, the clearly-delineated end phenomena of Objectives, and the predictable negative result of overrunning Objectives past their purpose and end phenomena, what must be the purpose and end result of the Miscavige Objectives policies? In practice, it is the creation of suggestible, deployable agents. People who are willing to, and who do, forfeit and surrender unto Scientology Inc. their children's future education funds, their retirement funds, and even the mortgages on their homes. The end products are mentally and spiritually broken people.

There are only a few alternatives for people caught in this ugly, repeating cycle:

1. Learn to put on a happy face while paying up to several hundred dollars an hour for the privilege of being led around a room, complying with meaningless orders.
2. Decide you are really messed up, and prove it to the church and yourself by acting messed up while complying – a means of justifying to oneself the tremendous wasted time and money.
3. Get the hell out and never look back.
4. Get the hell out, find a caring Independent Scientology auditor and get yourself rehabilitated (simple procedure) back to the point where you actually did attain the intended end phenomena.

Understanding the purpose and the expected end phenomena of Objectives is key. Lack of understanding of what all those exercises are intended to produce made the bad result possible in the first place.

CHAPTER SIX

GRADES

Grades are the heart and soul of Scientology. They are the compendium of solutions to what L. Ron Hubbard termed the barriers to living. Theoretically, a person could erase his reactive engram bank to attain the state of Clear and be not much better off than when he embarked on his journey. Sure, he would not be reactive. He would not be taking post-hypnotic commands from a hidden, out-of-control portion of the mind. But he would not necessarily be much wiser about life, because he would not fully understand how he got himself into the reactive mind trap in the first place. Absent outside influence, he would likely and merrily, if unwittingly, get busy building himself a doozy of a new reactive mind.

The Grades are much akin to classic schools of Zen Buddhism wherein the Master asks the student profound questions, and in the course of contemplating the answers, the student discovers all manner of revelations. But the Scientology Grades are far more organized, directed and certain. The preclear is asked a question or given a direction to recall something. The question is designed to lead to a revelation which unlocks or releases mental energy and mass. The question or command is given and answered over and over, until such time as a new realization about life occurs – called a 'cognition' in Scientology. These cognitions are really the wisdom one attains through Scientology auditing. The auditing process is designed such that when skillfully applied by an auditor, the cognitions come easily and more rapidly, each building on others to uncover and rehabilitate the thetan's abilities.

So well designed and organized are the processes that each Grade has a predicted ability gained, which is routinely achieved by a good auditor and willing preclear. Those end phenomena are outlined in chapter one of this book. David Miscavige's Scientology Inc., however, has corrupted the Grades in a number of ways. First, Miscavige has a penchant for attempting to put all of Scientology on automatic pilot. He wants the whole show to roll with no individual decision points or the judgment of any pesky humans getting in the way. Given that Grades deal with the very essence of life, and seek to increase an individual's self-determinism, judgment, wisdom and ability, Miscavige's aberration wreaks havoc at this level of the Bridge.

During much of the '80s and 2000s, Miscavige was on a kick to the effect that every single process listed (and there are many dozens at each Grade) must be run on every single preclear. This resulted in much the same deleterious effect as we outlined concerning Objective Processes in the last chapter: overrun. The felony is compounded when one considers a severe injunction L. Ron Hubbard laid down about Grades processes in particular. This was, "If it doesn't read, don't run it." Or the converse, only run what reads. 'To read' means that when consulting the preclear's understanding of the question or command, the e-meter needle indicates mental energy or mass is connected with the subject the process covers. That indication is given by an instantaneous reaction of the indicator needle on the meter. If the question doesn't read, it means this is not a fruitful or productive area for that preclear to delve into. Delving into an area that is not charged (containing mental energy and mass) creates mental energy and mass. Repeated too often, auditing winds up creating precisely that which it was designed to alleviate: mental mass. And that spells classic Black Dianetics.

Scientology Inc. auditors, particularly during the '80s and 2000s, were grooved into compliance with Miscavige's whims, and many preclears paid for it with bad experiences on the Grades. The '90s and 2010s were periods where Miscavige pendulum-swung in reaction to the very Grades arbitraries he himself had forcefully implemented in the '80s and 2000s. It seems as though Miscavige keeps capitalizing on the limited lifespan of Scientologists within the church, and the gullible state his practices apparently create among those who do stay.

In the 1980s, Miscavige presented himself (with many bells and whistles) to Scientologists as the savior who had figured out that people should be required to run every single Grade process. Then, in the '90s, he re-appeared as the brilliant mind who had spotted that very same practice as oppressive, and reinstituted short-cut Grades. Still later, in the early 2000s, as the "only real friend of Ron Hubbard," he "discovered" shortened, 'quickie Grades' were in vogue, and reinstituted lengthy running of every process. Finally, and most recently, in 2010 Miscavige retro-fitted himself as the same 1990s genius who recognized Grades must be streamlined and cut short.

So on Grades processes alone Miscavige has managed to keep himself in business as the cop – responsible for catching and correcting himself as the cat burglar – at least three times. The net result of it all is that corporate Scientology case supervisors and auditors are in a perpetual state of confusion as to what is the Miscavige formula de jour for Grades.

Miscavige's latest kick on shortened or 'quickie' Grades has resulted in unprecedented disaster as far as results of

Scientology auditing are concerned. One of the most reviled sins enumerated by L. Ron Hubbard was the practice of 'quickie Grades.' Every Scientology course of study begins with the same Hubbard Policy Letter, entitled *Keeping Scientology Working*. Hubbard ordered that this Policy Letter be placed as the first item of every course because, Hubbard noted, through neglect of its dictates in the '60s and '70s, "'Quickie grades' entered in and denied gain to tens of thousands of cases."

The only other Policy Letter likewise appearing at the beginning of every Scientology course, as ordered by Hubbard himself, is entitled *Technical Degrades*. In it, he reiterates: "The puzzle of the decline of the entire Scientology network in the late '60s is entirely answered by the actions taken to shorten time in study and in processing by deleting materials and actions." That very Policy Letter announces to all Scientologists that boasting of speed of auditing results encourages such quickie practice, and therefore such boasting would henceforth be considered an act of Treason and a High Crime.

Here is more on what Hubbard felt about quickie Grades:

'Quickie grades,' instead of making fortunes for one and all, crashed the whole Scientology network. BECAUSE QUICKIE RESULTS ARE LAZY AND DISHONEST. Let's just face up to the facts of life! Selling out the integrity of the subject for a buck wrecks the subject.

In the following passage, Hubbard gives an estimation of time and effort a single Grade should require:

A cognition at lower levels is not necessarily an ability regained. Thirty or forty cognitions on one lower level might add up to (and probably would) the realization that one is free of the whole subject of the level.

A cognition, or new realization about life, is what signifies an individual process has been completed. A definite ability regained demarks completion of an entire grade or level of the Bridge. So when Hubbard talks of 30 to 40 cognitions, he is expecting 30 or 40 processes to be run for each or any of the Grades (ARC Straightwire through Grade 4) in order for the preclear to really achieve the ability outlined for each Grade. In the face of what Hubbard's designs and intentions for the Grades were, let us consider the promotional materials emanating from corporate Scientology's headquarters since 2010. Here is an actual quote from Scientology Inc.'s promotion for results at their highest service organization, called Flag, also called their "mecca of technical perfection:"

An elderly lady, who has been stalled on the lower Bridge for several years, started on her Grades two weeks ago. When she was told to come and do her Grades at Flag and that, "Yes, you can do your Grades!" – she worked it out to go in session daily and she completed ARC SW, Grade 0, Grade 1, Grade 2 and is now on Grade 3.

First, quite obviously the mecca institutionally is committing treason and high crimes for boasting of speed of delivery of Grades. But let us look closer. In two weeks, a woman has allegedly completed four Grades and embarked on a fifth. Let's take the median of Hubbard's estimation of processes required to complete a Grade, 35. For a number of technical reasons, it would be impossible to run more than five Grade processes in a single day. That is because the effects of cognitions on Grades are cumulative and, if well audited, the preclear will become so extroverted that auditing time would be wasted trying to re-introvert his attention when in such a state (a prohibited practice in the first place). When such a state of extroversion occurs (which should come easily, after four or five major cognitions in a single day), a person is supposed to be given the day off to go enjoy his or her new perspectives and viewpoints, and to re-orient himself or herself to the world with these heightened spiritual awarenesses.

So at five processes a day, it would take seven days minimally to meet what Hubbard considers it ought to take for a person to complete a Grade. One would have to assume that the mecca does not give that person space and time to enjoy and re-acquaint with the world after having achieved the end phenomena of the full Grade. Further, if a Grade is run the way Hubbard prescribed it be run, positive spiritual phenomena would be present after several straight days of any auditing, and this would require the person be given as much time off between sessions as he or she wished – be that days, weeks, months or even years.

Let's just ignore all that and assume the mecca puts the woman back into the chair for the next Grade with no rest or respite – which is what they would have to have done to attain the time results they boast of. Under Hubbard's estimation of the care and effort it takes to achieve the ability of a Grade, it would take the person another week to complete a second Grade. At that point, given the continuous, intensive, uninterrupted nature of the auditing, it would be an impossibility that the preclear was not ready for an extended break. Unless, of course, the auditing was something less than standard – that is, less than as we have described it is supposed to be delivered, herein.

Let's put all that aside and examine the mecca's claims further. The mecca not only did not take seven days per Grade, with rest points in between Grades. It did two and a half grades in a single week, and another two and a half in the ensuing week. And so, in context, the mecca's claims should not be taken as brags to their having achieved Hubbard's standards, but rather as admissions that they thumb their noses at Hubbard's core philosophy. They don't want their preclears becoming more self-determined and spiritually aware. They want them "done" and back into the finance office, writing bigger checks for the next, more expensive levels.

Some might consider some of this criticism a tad nuanced, particularly since I have not taken the time to string together and cite the numerous Hubbard writings and lectures this quickie Grade mentality violates. So let us take another more obvious Flag mecca of technical perfection promotion, of recent vintage, to drive the point home:

Kathy ****** came to Flag on 4 July 2009, ready to start Grade II. She was gotten right into session and completed Grade II on 8 July. She then completed Grade III on 10 July.

Four days to achieve Grade 2. Another two days to achieve Grade 3. Any standard auditor or case supervisor knows these numbers, four days for Grade 2 and two days for Grade 3, are just plain criminal mathematics. Kathy has been cheated and taken advantage of – and no doubt will pay for it at the upper reaches of the Bridge. When you climb from a faulty foundation, you cannot climb very safely. There is another thing that is fairly predictable about Kathy's future in Scientology Inc. That is, while Kathy struggles with figuring out why those abilities gained don't seem to stick with her, she will be fleeced of every dollar and everything she owns along the rocky road she is being sent down. Perhaps that sheds light on why Scientology Inc. has institutionalized quickies grades.

What happened with Kathy, and worse, it is becoming standard operating procedure in the corporate Scientology network. Here is another recent promotional piece boasting of quickie Grades and claiming they are done in this fashion routinely:

At Flag people are moving up The Bridge faster than ever before. You can go to Flag at ARC SW case level and come home Grade IV complete in under 2 weeks. We are doing this on a regular basis.

That is five, if not six, Grades in less than two weeks. The mecca of Scientology has apparently become the mecca of desecration of L. Ron Hubbard and the technology of Scientology.

For those newly on the Grades or resuming them outside Scientology Inc., something ought to be known about the existing, lengthy Grade checklists. The fact is that L. Ron Hubbard did advise that the Grades checklists be a thorough compilation of every process he ever developed on each particular Grade. However, it was never intended that every single one of them be run on every person. As noted earlier, a cardinal rule in Scientology auditing is to run only those processes that read. Some of the Grade processes on the checklists are near duplicates of other processes on the checklists. A smart auditor or case supervisor would not robotically prescribe every process for every preclear. After running several initial processes, they would take heed of what the preclear was saying and experiencing. If the preclear had a huge release on an area covered by four pages of potential processes on that area, the case supervisor and auditor might move on to later sections of the checklist, addressing another area. To robotically check every process on the checklist could wind up grinding and introverting a preclear. An honestly-trained auditor and case supervisor who understand Hubbard's writings on case supervision would have no confusion on this – as long as they weren't under duress of enforcement of Miscavige's latest arbitrary pronunciamentos within Scientology Inc.

Grades are a pleasure to deliver and receive, providing the auditor and case supervisor grasp the technology and apply it sensibly – and, most importantly, with no other motive or intention than having the preclear truly and completely make each Grade.

CHAPTER SEVEN

CONFESSIONAL

Grade 2 of the Scientology Bridge deals with the Christian principle of the Golden Rule (treat others as you would have others treat you), the Hindu concept of Karma, and the Islamic idea of Kismet. I recognize that this statement alone could spark a debate that might never end, among religionists and atheists alike. But to a Scientologist who reaps the fruit that is attainable on Grade 2, all questions about the determination of her own fate and how she will get along with her neighbors and fellow human beings are quite satisfactorily answered. And the answers to those profound issues are supplied by the preclear herself.

At Grade 2, one deals primarily with the confronting and disclosing of one's transgressions against others. In the course of doing this, one finds that one has entrapped oneself, by tying up large portions of available attention in attempts to keep one's own shortcomings secret from others. The original idea in Dianetics was to address what had been done to the preclear to bring about the state she was in – and many Scientology processes are similarly directed. At Grade 2, one is more focused on what one has done to others.

Hubbard calls this type of auditor focus 'auditing the preclear at cause.' That is, the auditor directs the preclear to deal with what he has done to cause his own lessened state of awareness and ability. According to Hubbard, 'auditing the preclear at cause' – addressing his violations of his own understanding of right and wrong – is the most powerful Scientology processing there is. I have seen this manifested over and over. I have seen many people walking around in a crippled fashion, convinced that other people and the world at large are the cause of the hostilities and sufferings that burden them. On this Grade, these people lose those hostilities and sufferings, along with their "I'm a victim" outlooks on life. Facing up to, venting, and taking responsibility for one's own sins often converts a "glass-half-empty" type of individual into a "glass-half-full" one. Technically, the process assists a person to fully see how the Overt Act-Motivator Sequence (see Chapter One) has taken charge of his or her life, to one degree or another. It helps one transcend that vicious cycle.

Confession has been recognized as a powerful force for resurgence of a person's spiritual health for many centuries. It has been understood as such and applied by a number of religions and philosophies, and even by friends, parents and mentors. Unfortunately, the practice has been so abused by so many takers of confessions for so long, that the very discussion of the subject alone makes a lot of people queasy. When one invests his trust in another to hear his sins, and thus help him erase and free himself from their adverse effects, it is a sacred trust. When that trust is betrayed, as it often has been, it has devastating effects on the person so cheated. He learns that the only "safe" thing to do is to trust no one, and cling harder to his secrets and transgressions.

By doing so, he constructs a figurative wall, adversely affecting his relations with others and with the world at large. Less communication and less perception result in less awareness, and less affinity and reality with one's fellows. It is a dwindling spiral resulting in more hostility and suffering for the individual.

When a person is safe to vent his or her secrets, and does so thoroughly, two things become evident to the auditor. The first is that virtually everyone who engages in the process and carries it through to completion requires no discipline or punishment to mend his ways. After he is assisted in confronting that which he "forgot" in an attempt to ease his own conscience, a being naturally corrects his own behavior. To an auditor, this is one of the clearest proofs that spiritual beings are basically good by nature. Second, a person so processed is noticeably more communicative, perceptive, bright, alive, and active in life.

Hubbard recognized all of this, and lectured extensively on these ideas. He distinguished the Scientology confessional from other similar practices in two respects which, when adhered to, took the process to new levels of effectiveness. First was the inclusion of the e-meter. The e-meter's effectiveness at reading just below the level of the preclear's awareness assisted the preclear in uncovering areas of transgressions he had tried hard to forget, and had successfully forgotten. The levels of relief and heightened awareness experienced by preclears when directed by auditors to such buried and forgotten incidents are remarkable.

The second distinction was the Scientology auditor's training in the practice of compassion and understanding during sessions, never evaluating for or invalidating his preclear (forms of passing judgment). This factor was bolstered by a several-year track record of Scientology auditors consistently adhering to a code which, from the earliest days of Dianetics, prohibited the reporting or use of details disclosed in any auditing session for any other purpose than planning the preclear's future sequence of auditing. The following excerpt from a 1960 lecture by

Hubbard illustrates the importance he placed on the matter of Scientology organizations living up to that trust:

Well, this meant, essentially, that the preclear had to be willing to talk to the auditor. Well now, several things have to be guaranteed before this takes place. And one of the things that has to be guaranteed is that the preclear has some security in talking to the auditor that that information not be falsely used. Isn't that right?

[Audience: Yes.]

So this leaves us with an organizational responsibility heavier and bigger than we have ever had in the past. We've now got to go all out and make sure that a certificate means, wherever it is to be found, that confidence can be reposed in the person as a confidant. Isn't that right?

[Audience: Yes. Uh-huh.]

That organizationally, the information passing over organizational channels and so forth is inviolate – we have to be able to guarantee that, right?

[Audience: Right.]

During the development of the technology of confessional auditing and in its original practice, all transgressions confessed were absolutely and unconditionally forgiven by the auditor. As the years passed, for a variety of reasons, the guarantee that the preclear's security in confiding in the auditor came to be held less and less inviolate. Organizational concerns began to creep into and alter the technology, and those essential absolutes and unconditionals began to erode.

First was Hubbard's introduction of an exception to the rules of confession. That was that a confessional was sacred, and anything confessed was absolutely forgiven, except when it was an act that might affect the security of the organization. This led to auditors recording the details of confessed sins and reporting them to other church authorities when they were considered matters of concern to the survival of the organization.

Next entered the practice of using the confessional process for a purpose other than the benefit of the preclear. 'Security checks' were introduced. A security check was confessional procedure used to determine whether a Scientologist is worthy of trust by the organization. During the '60s and '70s the use of security checks proliferated for organizational security, justice, and disciplinary purposes. During Hubbard's life, with his continuing day-to-day influence on the operation of churches of Scientology, the increasingly-frequent use of security checking was tolerated. Apparently the tremendous relief and increases in perception and ability the auditing occasioned outweighed the embarrassments that security, justice and disciplinary uses wrought. But in the early '80s, as Hubbard withdrew from the church, and particularly after his 1986 death, the security check became an increasingly oppressive tool.

The e-meter began to be used more and more as an investigative tool. By the mid-1990s, David Miscavige had instituted the training of investigators – who were not even trained as auditors – to use e-meters for the purpose of interrogating suspects in internal investigations. By the early 2000s, Scientologists at all levels were routinely being hauled in by such investigators, ordered to pick up the e-meter electrodes, and interrogated for transgressions, crimes and even unacceptable thoughts they might be harboring (most specifically for such thoughts concerning David Miscavige).

For the past 20 years, security checking has been interjected at every level of the Scientology Bridge, with an ever-increasing array of pretexts to justify its misuse. The effects have been disastrous. Its original intended use at an early stage of the Bridge (Grade 2) can result in an individual transcending and freeing herself from the effects and continued entrapment of the Overt Act-Motivator Sequence. However, Scientology Inc.'s obsession with security checking has thoroughly programmed Scientologists to believe that the Overt Act-Motivator Sequence is ever-present, incomprehensible, invincible and inescapable. A Scientology Grade which once routinely proved to preclears the truth of Scientology's premise that a spiritual being is basically good, has been destroyed. In its place are ever-present e-meter interrogations, which drive home the (manifestly false) idea that not only are spiritual beings basically bad, they aren't ever going to be good – at least not through application of Scientology.

When a person is overrun on confessional auditing, just as with any other overrun, the individual begins to accumulate mental mass. That mental mass takes someone from a state of lightness of spirit and mind to one of heaviness and seriousness. When a person is repeatedly subjected to security checking on particular areas of concern to the organization, the person's attention is fixated more and more on those areas.

The preclear is subjected to unrelenting questions and demands that she find and divulge transgressions against those organizational concerns. This comes with the not-so-subtle implication that she must have such transgressions. She can only proceed by breaking down under this applied other-determinism and agreeing that the things she is being prompted to confess to constitute overt acts. This overrides the original Scientology definition of an overt act – an action that violates a person's own conception of right and wrong.

In this wise, a new moral code is imposed upon individuals, covertly and against their own determinisms. It is exacerbated by repeated questioning about the individual's failure to report on other Scientologists. After a while, a corporate Scientologist modifies her behavior accordingly, in order to avoid more security checks. She not only edits her own behavior and thoughts, she attempts to do the same with Scientologist friends and family members, so that she does not get into trouble for overlooking such transgressions of others. Thus, a process that was originally intended to free a person from the self-imposed mental prison she has created by her own inability to live up to what she considers right and ethical conduct becomes reversed. The preclear is instead forced to agree to a new mental prison, imposed by the organization based on what it decrees to be right or wrong. In short, the process replaces a person's native judgment with a new judgment of its own. In practice, it is a dark and painful operation, making a person less self-determined and more other-determined.

It seems that the only solution open to corporate Scientologists to cope and carry on within their culture is to become moralists. Moralists who enforce on self and others morals which have been implanted. If corporate Scientologists police their own conduct fastidiously enough, and interfere enough with the behavior and conduct of their fellows, they reckon they might be spared the cost, embarrassment and pain of being ordered to further batteries of security checks. In fact, that is the only behavior that does avoid continual, expensive, and degrading security checks in corporate Scientology.

This is yet another example of Scientology Inc.'s reversal of end product. Confessional technology was developed with the purpose to help an individual recognize she is the cause of her own destiny – and it has a long history of realizing that purpose. This priceless technology has been twisted and corrupted to the point where now the individual winds up with her destiny blueprinted and dictated by the church.

These blueprints are enforced through a related – and now similarly corrupted – technology of Scientology: the technology of ethics.

CHAPTER EIGHT

ETHICS

L. Ron Hubbard's development of Scientology ethics in the 1960s was perhaps the realization of one of the remedies he referred to in his 1950s lectures on Black Dianetics. With the advent of ethics technology, he created tools that could help an individual live by a higher ethic. Hubbard described ethics as 'reason' in contemplation of one's own survival, and resultant behavior that forwards one's survival while also enhancing the survival of as many others as possible. He described ethics as a personal thing, not something that could, or ought to be, enforced upon one by any individual or group. The enforcement of right conduct upon others, he noted, was not ethics at all, but instead a group's operation, properly labeled 'morals.' Morals are rules a group uses to keep members in line. Ethics is the self-imposed demonstration of personal integrity.

Upon his initial development of Scientology ethics, Hubbard made a clear distinction: Scientology was not interested in enforcing morals; Scientology was focused on helping a person to become more ethical. Hubbard created some very workable methodologies which a person could apply to himself, in order to live a life that brought better survival for himself and for those living within his sphere of influence. Application of ethics amongst Scientologists helped create auditors who obtained more certain and stable auditing results, and preclears and students who progressed up the Bridge more easily and with better results. That was Hubbard's aim in developing a technology of ethics in the first place.

Like the philosophy of Scientology itself, ethics was based on infinity-valued logic. That is, there are no absolutes, but instead gradients – potentially an infinity of them. There is no absolute right or wrong. Instead, there are infinite grades of relative rightness and wrongness. Understanding this, Hubbard developed a formula an individual could apply to any question in the sphere of ethics. That formula is simply that the optimum solution to any given situation is the one that brings about the greatest good for the greatest number of dynamics. The dynamics are eight arbitrary divisions of life, against which one can evaluate the optimum solution to any problem. The dynamics are:

1st Dynamic: The urge to survive as the individual himself, the spirit, his identity, his body, his possessions.

2nd Dynamic: The urge toward survival of, and as a member of, a family unit, including through sex and the rearing of children.

3rd Dynamic: The urge toward survival of, and as a member of, a group.

4th Dynamic: The urge toward survival of, and as a member of, Humankind.

5th Dynamic: The urge toward survival as a part of the group of all living things. This includes human beings, animals and plants.

6th Dynamic: The urge toward survival of, and as a part of, the physical universe (MEST: matter, energy, space and time).

7th Dynamic: The urge to survive as a participant in the spiritual universe (the universe of thetans, as opposed to matter, energy, space and time).

8th Dynamic: The urge to survive as, and as one relates to, the Creator – God or Infinity.

If one were to evaluate his courses of action against the standard of "what solution brings the greatest survival to the greatest number of dynamics?" it is easy to see that one would likely be a fairly positive force among his fellows. Hubbard devised a number of other formulas that break down how to put such solutions into action more effectively. But none of those formulas have the slightest possible positive effects if the pure, simple initial evaluation – 'greatest good for the greatest number of dynamics' – is not first put into play.

Most Scientologists will attest to having satisfactorily sorted out all manner of life problems through application of Scientology ethics. So workable is this technology that there are many non-Scientologists who, introduced to nothing else Scientological but its ethics, will attest to the same. Over time, however, the simplicity and power of Scientology ethics has been inverted, with many less-desirable results.

The first and biggest rub that began to spoil the simplicity of the optimum solution formula was introduced fairly early on in the development of Scientology ethics. The fundamental virus that ruined the workability of Scientology ethics was overt and covert tampering with the original 'greatest good' formula itself. For the formula to work, it is necessary to give each of the eight dynamics equal weight. That is, no single dynamic has any more value than any other dynamic, when contemplating an optimum solution. If one gives any one dynamic more value or influence than any other, the solution arrived at will be something other than what is optimum for the greatest number of dynamics. It more often than not would result in a solution that harmed more dynamics than it assisted.

Almost from the outset, the Scientology Inc. culture took for granted that since Scientology itself was the provider of the ultimate solution to survival across all dynamics, the organization – or group – that represents and forwards Scientology is more important than any other dynamic. Thus, from the mid-'60s to the present, the "3" on the keyboard of the calculator of optimum solutions has been permanently held down (Scientology Inc. representing the third dynamic). This has skewed every optimum-solution calculation attempted by Scientologists since.

As with virtually every other potential glitch in Scientology, the problem escalated exponentially after L. Ron Hubbard passed away in 1986. Granted, the problem has been there since the advent of Scientology ethics. But during the past three decades the problem has taken on such dimensions that it has effectively destroyed Scientology Inc., and many lives along the way. Currently in Scientology Inc. practice, the third dynamic is not just given more value than any other dynamic. It has taken on so much weight that in a corporate Scientologist's optimum-solution calculations, the "3" trumps all other dynamics combined. Let us examine the consequences.

Use of the optimum solution contemplation formula (which is the basis for and the sine qua non of Scientology ethics) has effectively been cancelled in Scientology Inc. It has been replaced with this one-dimensional – and more often than not, destructive – linear, insane thinking: "What is best for Scientology Inc.?"

'Reason,' as L. Ron Hubbard first defined 'ethics,' has become the prohibition of reasoning. Self-determinism, the restoration of which is the goal of all Scientology processes, has been replaced by the enforcement of group-determinism. In short, a culture whose members once reveled in the restoration of their liberty to think freely is now forced to think "our way or the highway," "the ends justify the means," and "by any means necessary."

In precisely this manner, ethics in Scientology has been replaced by enforcement of Scientology Inc. morals. The morals in play are the policies and mores of Scientology Inc. Those morals have evolved over the past three decades, increasingly influenced and dictated by the arbitrary decisions of one, single, rather ruthless individual. That one person is Scientology Inc. Chairman of the Board, David Miscavige. Here are some of the most commonly observed, tacitly-enforced tenets of Miscavige's new moral code within Scientology Inc.:

• A critic of Miscavige or Scientology Inc. must be depowered and destroyed by any means necessary. Image is everything when it comes to Miscavige and the corporations.

• Truth, if its disclosure might cause the slightest public relations harm to Scientology Inc. or to Miscavige, must be suppressed by any means necessary. Image is the only thing.

• Money into Scientology Inc. coffers is the most important product of Scientology Inc. The provenance of said funds is immaterial, and to question the means by which they were obtained is a punishable offense.

- It is acceptable and encouraged to use fraud, deceit, lies and threats against Scientologists to obtain ever-increasing sums of money for Scientology Inc.

- If anyone is dissatisfied with service received at any Scientology Inc. outlet, a staff member's first duty is to make the dissatisfied member believe the dissatisfaction was caused by the member himself. Scientology processes and technologies – including, but not limited to, auditing, security checking and ethics – are to be used cleverly to create this result in the minds of those expressing dissatisfaction.

- One overlooks all faults and corruption of higher-ups in Scientology Inc. Severity of repercussions for reporting or protesting corruption are directly proportional to the height on the organization chart of the corruption.

- One's level of ethics can be gauged by the magnitude of crime one will commit in order to protect the crimes of Miscavige and Scientology Inc. from disclosure.

- One may not read or listen to anything about Scientology – and least of all about David Miscavige – that is not officially published or broadcast by the church. Punishment is so severe for having done so that corporate Scientologists have resorted to extraordinary measures to avoid such, including staying away from the Internet entirely, and being careful not to watch or listen to the news.

- It is ethical behavior to snitch on your spouse, children, parents, co-workers and friends. It is unethical behavior not to immediately snitch on them when they are seen to violate the morals listed here.

- One must stay attuned to the list of personal, sexual, and group activities that are currently considered unacceptable or sinful. These vary with Miscavige's regressing predilections. Ignorance of this ever-shifting wind is not a defense for any transgression.

At first blush, one might believe there are exaggerations in the examples given. In fact, these are derived from hundreds of reports of former Scientology Inc. staff and members. These were listed as the most commonly reported. If one were to objectively observe his own experience, and investigate the experiences of his peers, he would find that these are, in reality, Miscavige's first Ten Commandments. They are ruthlessly enforced at all levels of corporate Scientology.

Since 1996, Miscavige has made it unalterable policy that the very top levels of the church, and all positions that enforce ethics within the Scientology Inc. network, must be manned by "young people" who have not been "corrupted" by veterans' views or influence on the subject of Scientology. Miscavige has directed that candidates be inexperienced in worldly matters, have the least formal education possible, and have little to no training and experience with Scientology auditing. He wants and gets impressionable minds – blank slates on which to draw his programs.

Many recent defectors have related one variation or another of the following scenario of how ethics is applied in Scientology Inc. A middle-aged woman, who had spent the past 30 years donating every available penny she earned to continue on up the Bridge, is found through security checking to have opened a bank account for retirement, which she has kept secret from the church. The woman is ordered to report to the "Ethics Officer" at the church's mecca in Clearwater, Florida. When she arrives, she is met by a cold, unfriendly 17-year-old boy in a naval uniform. The boy directs her to a room where she is told to pick up the electrodes of an e-meter. There are two other adolescent "Ethics Officers" in the room. The door is shut and all three Ethics Officers hurl insults about the alleged criminality of the woman under interrogation. They demand to know her crimes, and when none are forthcoming they shout guesses like, "Are you reading about Scientology on the Internet?" "Are you masturbating?" "Are you hiding more money from the church?" and on and on. The three stare menacingly at the woman and then at the meter, to see if it reads. They make all manner of false accusations, and – not knowing how to use a meter, or that it is worthless under such oppressive circumstances – they claim it is reading in response to some of their accusations. This can go on for hours and hours. Ultimately, the troika forces the woman to disclose every asset she has access to, and extracts a promise of payment of the bulk of those assets to the church, in order to be spared more mental torture. This would be a fairly mild encounter with "Ethics," by comparison with the actual experiences of hundreds who have shared their own with me.

It is perfectly okay, even prescribed, to have specialists in the ethics discipline assist others in the use of Scientology ethics as a tool. But, as with any bit of Scientology technology, ethics cannot be enforced upon a person. To override a person's self-determinism is to lose the effectiveness of Scientology. It is no different with Scientology ethics.

Scientology ethics has become so perverted and bastardized in Scientology Inc. that one could write a number of books on that subject alone. But to go down that alley would be a waste of time. Virtually any bad effect caused through misapplication of Scientology ethics techniques is bad because it begins with a violation of Scientology ethics' first principle: ethics is simply contemplation of optimum survival across the dynamics. If one kept that in mind, and it informed one's purpose in applying virtually any tool or method of Scientology ethics, no complaints or deleterious effects would be created. Quite to the contrary.

I recently watched a movie that serves as a perfect, though unintended, example of how Scientology ethics was meant to be effectively applied. *Freedom Writers* is based on a true story. It tells of the experiences of a compassionate young woman who is determined to overcome barriers in educating a classroom full of "dead-end" kids. Most of the 9th graders in her class initially demonstrate an abject lack of ethics. They are gang members, drug abusers, drug dealers, thieves, and all-around misfits. The teacher, Ms. G, succeeds by making the children aware of, and participating in, their dynamics. This terminology is of course not used, and in fact Ms. G was not even following any prescribed course, let alone Scientology ethics. She was simply, step by step, doing what she considered the right thing to do.

She first makes the children aware of their own individual presence, behavior, appearance and conduct: the first dynamic. Next, she becomes familiar with their lack of any meaningful family life, and begins to substitute in the role of a parent – giving the children the idea there is such a thing as a family, the second dynamic. By spanning their attention that far, she is able to bring the students up to acknowledging the existence of one another – which leads to their considering themselves members of a group, the third dynamic. Part of that process involved breaking down ethnic prejudices within the class, which had prevented the students from bonding with one another as a group. That process had Ms. G and the students venturing into the realm of the fourth dynamic, giving the students an awareness of Humankind as a whole. Part of that process involved getting the students interested in issues facing all of humanity. As awareness of and involvement in each of these dynamics increased, each of these students made positive changes in their first and second dynamics. Ultimately, the students demonstrated a high level of ethics, and began to study in earnest. Many of them, once destined for addiction or death at an early age, went on to become the first members of their families ever to attend college.

Ms. G's story does not unfold quite as linearly as I have described. But the result and effect were there – Ms. G spanned each student's attention to awareness of dynamics they had not even known existed. The more aware and involved they became with more dynamics, the more informed by all dynamics their life choices became. It was clear to see that the process resulted in universally-understood concepts of goodness, healthiness, and wholesomeness being realized for the students, across all dynamics.

When a school board member in the film asks Ms. G whether she could replicate her accomplishments with a new, incoming group of students, she honestly answers, "I don't know." She was not quite aware of what the active ingredient of her success was. Aside from the manner in which she conducted herself (good, clean intention, compassion, understanding, patience and persistence), she did not know what had actually occurred with her students that had made them more decent, honest, intelligent people.

Ms. G was able to achieve what no other teacher had. Not by force, not by discipline and not by punishment. Only through compassion, inspiration and leadership was she able to achieve a new, high level of ethics among her students. So Ms. G, not knowing what she had done (increased awareness and responsibility of her students across the dynamics) only knew how she conducted herself vis-à-vis her students. Not knowing a thing about Scientology ethics, Ms. G demonstrated precisely how Scientology ethics works, and how it must be applied in order to work.

Freedom Writers should be an important pre-requisite study for anyone attempting to apply Scientology ethics to another. First, so that they can see the results attainable by helping another understand there are more dynamics than just the first, that happiness and survival depend upon this understanding, and that this understanding alone makes better people. Second, so that one can see how understanding is brought about. It is not by force, by policing, by punishment or by threat. It is only brought about by demonstrating care, and by increasing affinity, reality and communication.

It would do a lot of good for anyone affected by misapplication of Scientology ethics to watch *Freedom Writers*. For such people, there is another potential benefit, in addition to those already noted. You might see that the bulk of L. Ron Hubbard's contributions were in the organizing and codifying of workable things that many people have already discovered and done. Hubbard has stated as much – though admittedly he implied otherwise at other times, perhaps making the truth of the matter unclear. In either event, recognizing that truth is part of yet another remedy in the healing process for refugees from Scientology Inc. culture. That is, comparing what they learned in Scientology to similar applications and results in other walks of life. It could help mitigate the inculcated idea that unless every member of Humankind adopts everything Hubbard ever wrote, and applies it literally, every minute of the day, humankind is doomed. And that in turn might help them to get over the idea that the group "Scientology" should be the perpetually held-down 3 on the keyboard of the optimum solution computer.

CHAPTER NINE

SUPPRESSION

The most potent sub-study of Scientology ethics is that of the detection and handling of suppression in an individual's life. It also happens to be the most reviled body of work Hubbard ever penned. Ironically, Hubbard's perennial and harshest critics – leaders in the fields of psychiatry and psychology – over the last few decades have begun to parallel much of what Hubbard discovered on the subject in the 1950s and 1960s.

Hubbard began writing about the negative effects of the anti-social personality as early as 1951. His second major book, *Science of Survival: Prediction of Human Behavior*, presented a comprehensive system for plotting personality on an emotional scale, from which one could determine the most effective approach for raising any individual on that same scale. The anti-social type personality received special and repeated reference in *Science of Survival*, as Hubbard noted it was the toughest type to spot and, undetected, it wrought the greatest havoc in the lives of social personalities. As with the rest of Scientology, the sub-study of the prediction of behavior continued to evolve.

In the mid-1960s, Hubbard authored a series of essays which focused on the anti-social personality and the negative effects he brings into the lives of those he touches. Hubbard wrote that the mechanisms used by the anti-social personality to bring down others manifested themselves in a plethora of ways, many difficult to detect. The common denominator of the effect of such behaviors could be summed up in one word: suppression. Suppression plays out across a spectrum of forms – from overt and loud, such as violence, to covert and quiet, such as persistent cutting remarks and invalidation (convincing others that to hope and to strive are naïve and fruitless notions). Hubbard called a person who specialized in ruining the lives of others a 'suppressive person' or 'SP.' Hubbard labeled a victim of an SP a 'potential trouble source' or 'PTS.' Thus, 'PTS/SP' technology resulted – how to detect and handle suppression in one's life and help others to do the same.

Hubbard postulated that virtually all mistakes, accidents and illnesses were born out of suppression. This statement has come to be criticized as absolutist and arbitrary. Taken literally and out of context, as so many excerpts of Scientology are, by critics – and most unfortunately by corporate Scientologists themselves – it does seem rather extreme.

However, within the evolutionary context of an extensive body of work, 15 years in the making, it makes more sense than it seems to at first blush. Let's take a simple example to illustrate the inanity of the extremist interpretation. The corporate Scientologist and critic interprets the statement "all mistakes, accidents and illnesses stem from suppression" to mean that an individual who dropped a box of fragile crystal glasses must then be hauled in by a Scientology ethics officer to have his life extensively probed, in search of the mysterious suppressive person who is stealthily plotting to destroy the PTS fellow. Unfortunately, that is about how literally Scientology Inc. applies the idea.

By contrast, a sane Scientologist might utilize the datum to examine what in the fellow's environment may have influenced his accident/mistake. He might find that the 'suppressor' or 'cause' for the mishap was disorder in the storeroom. He replaces a light bulb and clears the passageway of such 'suppression' so that a similar accident won't recur. He doesn't need an auditor, an ethics officer, or a psychiatrist to figure that out for him. He simply applies what he learns, rather naturally and smoothly and to good effect.

However, when an individual is found to be experiencing an unreasonable number of accidents, injuries, illnesses and/or mishaps, a caring Scientologist might well want to assist the person so affected to examine whether there is someone in his life who is acting so as to create a frame of mind that seems to call for the illness-and-accident prone person to continually punish himself. That is, help him to cut through the fog an anti-social personality is so adept at constructing so as to obfuscate his own role in messing up the lives of others. The results of logical application of PTS/SP technology in such circumstances can be miraculous. Thousands have attested to such applications clearing up illnesses, healing injuries, ending a long series of seemingly never-ending mishaps, or making the gains they have made in Scientology more lasting and stable.

To pretend or argue that Hubbard was not fairly accurate when it came to describing the modus operandi and the behavioral characteristics of the anti-social personality or suppressive person is tantamount to denying the work that several mental health disciplines have carried out on the subject for several decades since. Psychiatrists and psychologists refer to the anti-social type suppressors of life by the terms 'psychopath' and 'sociopath.' The world's leading authority on the subject is Dr. Robert Hare. The checklist of characteristics of the psychopath developed by Hare, and more fully described in his several books on the subject, could have been compiled nearly verbatim from the works of L. Ron Hubbard between 1951 and 1967.

Probably the most readable and interesting description of how Hare's criteria manifest appears in Martha Stout's 2011 book *The Sociopath Next Door*. Stout is particularly credible, since her observations and summations are based on more than two decades of specializing in the healing of the victims of sociopaths. Another more entertaining account of the checklist was written by Welsh journalist Jon Ronson in *The Psychopath Test*. Both *Sociopath* and *Psychopath* are recommended to Scientologists, former Scientologists, critics and anyone else affected by or interested in Hubbard's work on the subject. If one engaging in this study hasn't already done so, he also ought to read Hubbard's *Science of Survival*.

In the mid-'60s, Hubbard suggested that approximately 2½ percent of the general population were of the anti-social variety. The Hare school of psychopathy puts the current percentage in America at 4. That is remarkably consistent, when one considers the latter is proffered nearly 50 years after Hubbard's guess, and when considering that the Hare school posits that our consumerist/capitalist society rewards and thus breeds an increase in occurrence of psychopathy. Stout's *Sociopath*, and writings of Hare himself, contend that sociopathy may well be the number-one unsolved problem threatening our civilization. Hubbard asserted the same 45 years ago.

Science of Survival has received extensive criticism for its assertion that anti-social personalities ought not to be afforded civil rights, but instead ought to be quarantined in order to protect potential victims from their evil doings. Mental health professionals have led that critical chorus for the past six decades. Hubbard wrote that passage after concluding that the anti-social personality was incapable of cure, since the anti-social personality was certain there was nothing wrong with himself, and that in fact it was "everybody else" who was insane and in need of extermination. Ironically, 60 years after *Science of Survival*, mental health professionals find themselves coming to the same conclusion, and struggling to put it in more socially acceptable, politically correct terms. Ultimately, as *Psychopath* makes clear, the mental health profession has, for six decades – and continues to this day – done precisely as Hubbard recommended in 1951. They commit sociopaths to institutions, and they go to great lengths to justify keeping them held against their constitutional and civil rights, indefinitely. Sure, they have attempted cures (from the benign to psycho-surgery, to electro-convulsive shock therapy, to even putting psychopaths on huge doses of LSD). But at the end of the day, in the year 2012, they have concluded they cannot cure a psychopath, and quarantine is the only answer.

Hubbard has been criticized roundly for noting that when a person is determined, beyond a shadow of a doubt, to be a vampire-personality sociopath, ruining the life of another individual, the latter had better disconnect from the former if he or she is interested in surviving and flourishing in life. 'Disconnect' means to entertain no further contact with the sociopath, to sever all communication with him. There is nothing objectionable to the mental health establishment with that advice. At least not according to Stout, who wrote:

The best way to protect yourself from a sociopath is to avoid him, to refuse any kind of contact or communication…The only truly effective method for dealing with a sociopath you have identified is to disallow him or her from your life altogether. Sociopaths live completely outside of the social contract, and therefore to include them in relationships or other social arrangements is perilous. (The Sociopath Next Door)

Where Hubbard and corporate Scientology got into trouble was in attempting to make the corporation the final and only adjudicator of who is and who is not a sociopath, and who must therefore disconnect from the person so labeled. In Scientology, that means labeled a 'suppressive person.' To exacerbate matters, Scientology Inc. began to enforce their 'disconnect' dictates with strong penalties applied for non-compliance. Hubbard complicated matters further when he made it a technical "fact" that when one non-complies with a directive to disconnect from a designated suppressive person then he himself becomes a suppressive person by virtue of that non-compliance. Logical findings – validated by mental health sciences in decades that followed – were ruined by such illogical thinking and enforcement.

A debate has raged for many years among former and independent Scientologists as to whether Hubbard's 'disconnect' dictates ought to be interpreted in this wise in the first place, whether he canceled them, and whether later in life he reinstituted them. That will be clarified in the later book exploring the whys for the demise of corporate Scientology. In either event, the controversy is becoming less relevant and more academic as the independent Scientology movement expands. One thing virtually all independent Scientologists seem to concur on is that no agency less than God has the right to tell a person with whom he or she may or may not communicate.

What is not in dispute is that corporate Scientology under David Miscavige for the past three decades has run a tight, ruthless "with us or against us" disconnect policy. It has gone far beyond the original prescribed pattern. That pattern began with thorough investigation to determine whether a person was technically a sociopathic, psychopathic, suppressive person. It included a justice apparatus for an individual so labeled to make his case to the contrary. Finally, it entailed the public declaration of the finding, which served as an advisory to Scientologists to steer clear of that person.

That system has degenerated into an oppressive, backward, witch-hunting culture where corporate Scientologists must always be on the alert not to make friends with someone who might not be in the best stead with the current Scientology bureaucracy, and most importantly with supreme leader David Miscavige. Unwritten, yet well understood and complied with, policies have emerged and taken strong hold. Miscavige is the originator or final arbiter of who gets declared suppressive. Rarely is such a determination made on the basis of an objective investigation. Justice procedures to curb any mistakes or abuses have been entirely removed from the line-up. Obtaining information about Miscavige or corporate Scientology from any other source than Miscavige-authorized propaganda is strictly prohibited. Scientologists who so much as read press accounts or information available on Internet sites about Scientology, and particularly about Miscavige, are disciplined, and if they do not erase such information from their very minds, they ultimately wind up declared suppressive persons.

When one considers the widespread practice of Black Dianetics being directed by Miscavige and being carried out at all levels of the corporate Scientology hierarchy as we are outlining herein, one can see the recipe for disaster rendered with such policies added into the mix. Should one object or even disagree with the reversal of Scientology processes to achieve domination and control, one is in danger of being declared a suppressive person. With that declaration comes the loss of contact with all Scientologists. For many, that means loss of contact with every member of his family, every business contact he has developed over years, every professional he consults (from lawyers and accountants to medical doctors) and every friend made over decades of participation in Scientology. It means effectively the overnight transmogrification from a human being into a contaminated member of some sub-human species.

If a Scientologist shows the slightest sign of considering that a declared suppressive person is anything other than radioactive, that Scientologist will be threatened with such treatment himself. For many years running, more people have been declared to be suppressive by reason of maintaining a connection to an alleged suppressive person, than have for having been independently adjudicated to fit the definition of an anti-social personality. Scientology Inc. has degenerated into a police-state culture that punishes guilt by association.

To even inadvertently demonstrate support of anyone associated with someone deemed suppressive by Scientology Inc. carries grave consequences for a corporate Scientologist. Consequently, corporate Scientologists must develop rather anti-social habits in order to stay aloof and unconnected to anybody who may be labeled suppressive by the organization. In my opinion, this is a major reason why outsiders increasingly have come to the conclusion that Scientologists are humorless, uptight and nosey, and that they act in a holier-than-thou manner. These personality flaws are inculcated as necessities for survival within the corporate Scientology culture.

Three decades of this McCarthy-era-style disconnect culture has also resulted in Scientologists becoming some of the most socially unconscious individuals around. Corporate Scientology promotes the social betterment activities of Scientologists in inverse proportion to Scientologists' worsening social tone-deafness. Thus, Miscavige runs a torture and concentration camp for managers of Scientology Inc. near Hemet, California, while celebrity Scientologists lend their talents to an ever-increasing stream of human rights promotional videos and events sponsored by the Los Angeles-based Scientology Celebrity Centre. Thus, we see Scientologist opinion leaders using Scientology facilities to back socially regressive, reactionary politics and candidates. Thus, we see second-generation Scientologist teenagers gleefully informing on their parents for not snappily conforming to the latest Scientology Inc. party line. Consequently those parents are declared suppressive and lose their families and careers overnight, while their snitching children are heaped with praise within. Meanwhile, Scientology Inc.

increasingly churns out propaganda about how it enhances family life.

With this cultural regression running unabated, the gains that the technology can deliver, many of which we cover in this book, are not only taken away, they are reversed to less enlightened states than many had when they approached Scientology to begin with. Take Grade 0 on the Bridge, for example. The Communication level. The official, expected ability gained at that Grade is stated as:

Willing for others to communicate to him on any subject. No longer resisting communication from others on unpleasant or unwanted subjects. Ability to communicate freely with anyone on any subject.

Under the duress of Scientology Inc.'s policies on 'disconnection', corporate Scientologists can become extremely wary of communicating with many categories of people.

Next let us consider the vaunted state of Clear. When Hubbard announced the achievement of routinely assisting people to attain the state, he described the end product in these terms:

It's simply making them more capable and more able, and increasing in particular (watch this carefully) their creativeness and increasing in particular their tolerance.

Tolerance? Tolerance is one of the last words an outside observer would use to describe a corporate Scientology Clear. And for good reason. Clears in Scientology Inc. culture must be extremely intolerant of any views or activities that do not align one hundred percent with the views and activities that David Miscavige espouses. Since Miscavige's views are decidedly bigoted, small-minded, aggressive, xenophobic, racist and sexist, the views of corporate Scientologists are evolving in a similar unhealthy direction.

Disconnection is being used with much the same result across the Scientology Bridge. The warped, intolerant, censorious application of the 'disconnect' policy systematically corrupts the self-determinism attained through auditing, and replaces it with a dutiful, careful, intolerant, and compliant attitude.

Compounding this madness is the purpose 'disconnect' has served over the past three decades. It has not served its original purpose, which was to protect the rights and sanity of honest people and allow them the opportunity to strive toward spiritual freedom without interference. Instead, since the rise of Miscavige in the early '80s, it has been used almost exclusively to prevent the free flow of information amongst Scientologists. It began with Miscavige using 'disconnect' to stomp out a fledgling movement that protested his ascent to the helm of Scientology Inc. Disconnection has been used ever since for the primary purpose of ensuring that evidence of Miscavige's subsequent crimes never becomes known to the population of Scientologists whose donations continue to make him wealthy. All of these facts have resulted in a movement that once prided itself on free thinking, freedom of information, and compassion for humanity, steadily deteriorating into a destructive cult.

Ironically, perhaps the best way to understand the most fundamental flaw in the Scientology system of dealing with the influence of sociopaths is to read a book that touches on corporate Scientology's vehement, costly protests against the alleged failure of the field of psychiatry to do the same. In *The Psychopath Test*, Ronson chronicles a member of corporate Scientology's Citizens Commission on Human Rights (a group established to "clean up the field of mental healing") and his quest to free an allegedly falsely labeled psychopath from a United Kingdom mental institution.

Ronson becomes fascinated with the apparent terrible injustice of "Tony's" (pseudonym) incarceration. As Ronson researches the matter in greater depth, he comes to find the Bob Hare psychopath test, or checklist, rather rational and workable. The more time Ronson spends with Tony, the more he begins to doubt the fellow's sanity against the psychopath test. Out of curiosity, Ronson puts the test to use on a businessman who is unrelated to the matter of Tony. When he completes the analysis, Ronson shares his condemning findings with a fellow journalist. His colleague points out that Ronson only spent a couple of hours with the target, and perhaps his journalistic skill of luring a target into making lurid admissions, and his preconceived notions of guilt, played a part in his finding. Ronson, in his honest and entertaining style, rides the rollercoaster of enthusiastic certainty to self-deprecating doubt in his own and others' use of the psychopath test.

Ultimately, Ronson causes the reader to consider that while there is a tremendous, accurate compilation of information that helps us detect sociopathy, can any one of us be trusted with the power to judge and sentence anyone else against that information? Are any of us worthy of the God-like power to condemn another to a life of quarantine and isolation? Do we, in wielding such a powerful tool of knowledge, tend to take on the characteristics of the sociopath when we sit in judgment?

Ronson seems to wind up in much the same place L. Ron Hubbard did when he published this statement: "I have come to find that man cannot be trusted with justice." While Hubbard persevered and constructed an elaborate system of justice intended to overcome that fatal flaw of humankind, for whatever reason, his lack of trust was proved justified by his own creation.

Ultimately, though, L. Ron Hubbard said that the only guarantee that one would not wind up on the receiving end of a sociopath's club was to understand how to identify one in the first place. And that conclusion was echoed by Martha Stout. The founder of Scientology and his long-time nemeses in the field of mental health ended up agreeing on one unifying principle: When it comes to the havoc others can wreak upon one's life, the best protection is the truth – know it, and it shall set you free.

And so my recommended remedy in dealing with the very real problem of sociopathy, or the suppressive person, is as follows:

• Learn for oneself how to evaluate the worthiness and value of one's fellows.

• Never forfeit your judgment to some authority, no matter how apparently wise and judicious, when it comes to judging the merits of others.

• Strive to be worthy of the trust of those you care about.

Where Hubbard and the psychiatrist and psychologist parted company fundamentally was in Hubbard's claim in the '60s that the anti-social personality could be cured. While it was a commendable intent, it might well have sown the seed that sprouted the vine that ultimately choked corporate Scientology to death. What followed was a complex schema of organizational policies that began a trend toward retaining anti-social personalities, rather than dismissing them. Concentration camps were established in several countries, for rehabilitating psychopaths who had somehow found their way into Scientology management. For decades, dozens of lawsuits and hundreds of news stories have pronounced the system guilty of perpetrating the wholesale violation of civil and human rights. To a large extent, the system helped to define Scientology in the minds of the public at large. Those asylums were set up, for the most part, to be run by the inmates. This resulted in many anti-social behaviors being accepted as correctable. Failing at such correction in a substantial percentage of cases, it resulted further in the recycling of uncorrected and unrepentant psychopaths throughout Scientology management.

Many anti-social policies and patterns developed over the next several decades within Scientology Inc. management. Over time, the sociopath camps became populated, more often than not, by social personalities who had been targeted by anti-social personalities who remained within the management structure. By the turn of the millennium, the camps routinely served to deter social personalities within Scientology Inc. management from blowing the whistle on anti-social behavior in the upper ranks of the organization.

The final result was foreseen by some, and in retrospect that is not surprising. Ultimately, and ironically, upon Hubbard's passing away in 1986, a man who could have served as a textbook case study in Stout's *The Sociopath Next Door* – not to mention the ne plus ultra anti-social personality, gauged against Hubbard's own published criteria – became the undisputed and unchallengeable supreme ruler of corporate Scientology. Perhaps therein lies the primary cause of the demise of Scientology Inc.

CHAPTER TEN

RIGHT AND WRONG

One major reason why corporate Scientologists cannot be trusted with justice is their inculcated obsession for being "right," while at the same time making other people wrong. This again is ironic, since Scientology includes a whole body of technology designed to help a person transcend this common human trait which makes relationships so difficult.

Those who survive the misapplication of the technologies of ethics and suppression covered in the last two chapters, and who remain within the corporate Scientology culture, must learn something well, in order to carry on. To survive within that closed society, one must learn to comfortably ignore all news media, all websites, and all friends, family and associates who might impart some of the facts we are discussing in this book. What is the most effective means for accomplishing that? The answer is to train oneself to consider that all news media, all websites, all friends, family and associates who do not agree one hundred percent with Scientology are not worthy of consideration. In other words, carry around an automatic consideration that such sources are wrong, while also considering that one's corporate-Scientology frame of mind is always right.

This is a form of what Dr. Robert Jay Lifton described as 'thought stopping' in his 1961 book, *Thought Reform and the Psychology of Totalism: A Study of "Brainwashing" in China*. Apparently, 1950s Communist China had it down to a science. They made the penalties for entertaining and sharing Western thought so gruesome that the population was required to develop a technique for keeping their minds free from such pesky notions taking hold. The communist authorities accomplished this by categorizing fields of thought, labeling them with a catch phrase such as "bourgeois thinking." Then they grooved the population in to reporting on evidence of such diseased thinking circulating. Finally, the authorities would punish the now identified minds from which such thinking emanated. After a while the people at large carried on effectively as slaves by stopping such thoughts from polluting their own minds. They stopped thought patterns in themselves by labeling and rejecting foreign notions as 'bourgeois thinking.'

Scientology as a culture has developed a number of such handy labels, which make a Scientologist feel comfortable, even superior and more pure, by shutting himself off from the fruits of information intake. The most important Scientology Inc. thought categorization labels that have evolved are as follows:

• Wog think. The term 'wog' comes from early Hubbard lectures wherein he borrowed an old British Empire pejorative term, which to the Brits meant a usually darker-skinned and presumably inferior native of one of Britain's many colonies and protectorates. (When challenged on his use of the demeaning term, a British officer is reported to have replied that 'wog' was merely short for 'Worthy Oriental Gentleman.') Hubbard redefined 'wog' to mean 'a non-Scientologist,' or 'someone who is not even trying' (not trying, that is, to find a way out of the misery of day-to-day humanoid existence). While the use of the term always fostered some level of 'us (Scientologists) vs. them (non- Scientologists)' attitude, since Hubbard's 1986 death it has developed into a damning slur and label of condemnation. The term "wog think" has eventually been redefined further as thought that conflicts in any way with the dictates and "wisdom" of David Miscavige. Virtually any idea originating outside the confines of Scientology Inc. is facilely dismissed with the label "wog think."

• Psych think. This label applies to any notion whose origin could be traced to, or be influenced even indirectly by, traditional mental health fields (psychiatry, psychology, psychotherapy, even New Age practices). Such ideas are not only rejected, they are to be feared and thus destroyed. Should such ideas manage to creep into the mind of a corporate Scientologist, Scientology Inc. culture teaches that one's eternal salvation is at risk. Hubbard's voluminous writings condemning the fields of psychiatry and psychology give ample credibility to the Scientology Inc. notion that such ideas could literally poison one's soul for eternity. The fact that much of Hubbard's rancor was vented in that direction in response to organized psychiatry's vicious condemnation of Dianetics and Scientology and, by extension, himself, is wholly lost on the corporate Scientologist. They are fundamentalists, and, just as radical Islamists insist that Mohammed's 1500-year-old cry for jihad must be taken literally in the here and now, corporate Scientologists insist that all psychiatrists and psychologists and their very disciplines must be obliterated. Mark my words: Scientology Inc. will present to Scientologists, as one of the first "proofs" of the dangers of reading this book, its references to, excerpts from and recommendations to read books written by mental health professionals.

- Reasonableness. Here is one of the most insidious developments of post-Hubbard corporate Scientology. Hubbard wrote a series of essays on the subject of logic, called the Data Series. In the Data Series, Hubbard noted that people who lack the power of simple observation are quick to invent data to explain away observed phenomena. For example, imagine a fellow encountering an apparently dead body on the sidewalk as he is walking home from work. For fear of getting involved as a potential witness, he quickly comes up with a "reasonable" explanation that serves as justification for looking the other way. He "reasons" it away by deciding, "Well, we're near a ball park and the fellow is probably napping after having gotten exhausted playing a tough game of ball." Hubbard called this justification process 'reasonableness.' By way of a long, circuitous route, during the Miscavige regime 'reasonableness' has come to mean a couple of things, both quite different from Hubbard's original definition. First, 'reasonableness' has come to mean 'demonstrated agreement with something destructive, like wog think or psych think.' A person guilty of 'reasonableness' in this sense can count on a lengthy stint with the ethics officer, to have his 'think' readjusted.

Second, particularly at the higher levels of management, 'reasonableness' means 'cowardice' and 'giving succor to the enemies of Scientology.' It is demonstrated by omission, in particular by the failure to punish someone severely enough for Miscavige's liking. The only cure for 'reasonableness' in Scientology Inc. management is the demonstration of 'unreasonableness' – which, in turn, has taken on the connotation of ruthlessness (which, to Miscavige's way of thinking, is a good thing). In Miscavige's presence, that translates into physical violence visited upon anyone who may have committed 'wog think' or 'psych think' in Miscavige's zone of influence. And so, just as with 'Newspeak' in George Orwell's *1984* ('Peace = War,' for example) along with 'wog think' and 'psych think,' the notion of 'reasonableness' has become a punishable offense in corporate Scientology.

These notions are deeply implanted in the minds of corporate Scientologists by yet another reversal of the technology of Scientology. Grade 4 is the final Scientology Grade before Clear or the OT levels. It is the culmination of 16 years of intensive research and practice by L. Ron Hubbard, identifying and overcoming the barriers to Clearing and to living. Grade 4 is the point of positive departure in his research. It is the point on the Bridge where focus on removing spiritual disabilities turned instead toward restoring and enhancing spiritual abilities. Here is where Hubbard claimed a person made the Grade when he demonstrated the following:

Moving out of fixed conditions into ability to do new things; ability to face life without need to justify own actions or defend self from others; loss of make-guilty mechanisms and demand for sympathy; can be right or wrong.

Whereas Grades 0 through 3 focused mostly on what others had done to the preclear, and what the preclear had done to others that ended up making the preclear less able, aware, and happy, Grade 4 shifted the focus onto what the individual had done to himself to limit his own potential. We find that primarily what he did to himself was to make decisions along the course of his life, which limited his abilities. By addressing the greatest source of his own limitations – his own responsibility for the decision-making process – a person is introduced to a future of unlimited possibilities.

The villain one conquers at Grade 4 is called the 'computation.' A 'computation' is defined as that aberrated evaluation and postulate (causative, decisional thought) that one must be in a certain state in order to succeed. An individual adopts false identities (called 'valences' in Scientology), and all the disabilities that come with them, during moments when his survival is threatened. These valences are held in place by the evaluations and postulates (computations) we make in those stressful moments. The computations apparently worked in some dire moment. They worked so well that we keep them in place, on automatic, not even aware that we continue to automatically activate that "successful" earlier conclusion throughout the rest of our lives, to our own detriment. Computations are always illogical, sometimes even so contradictory as to seem absurd when discovered.

Let us draw a dramatic example for purpose of illustration. A young man is sent to the front lines in a war. He is bombarded and shot at from all angles. He sees comrades about him falling like flies. It is a mass confusion accompanied by serious incoming threats to his survival. Logic is abandoned. He has no one he can communicate to about the problem he faces. He sees a fellow soldier madly dash from his foxhole across the battlefield, firing his rifle at the enemy all the way, to a rock shelter 50 yards ahead. Our soldier half-reactively reckons that the fellow who made it across was acting as if he had decided he would fight to the death. Our soldier decides likewise, adopting the valence of the fellow who is momentarily surviving. He runs across the battlefield with all-out abandon, on the idea that deciding to fight to the death was the winning answer. Our soldier and the solider he emulated continue on in this vein several more times, fighting while fully willing and expecting to die. To their surprise, they do not die. Instead, the enemy flees. Both soldiers are honored and promoted in rank. Our soldier, who up to that time had not often succeeded at any life endeavor, is now a hero for the first time in his life. He makes a computation that "the best way to survive is to fight to the death." It sure worked when he applied it the first time.

Not quite consciously, our soldier continues to act out the winning computation throughout the rest of his life. Whenever he faces a stressful situation that he considers a threat to his survival he instinctively fights to the death.

Complications ensue in a peacetime society. When our soldier is threatened by a drunk in a bar, his response is to beat the man to a bloody pulp. He is charged with aggravated assault and battery. Part of the insidious nature of such computations is that they compel an individual to prove himself right with them, while making others who oppose him wrong. Thus, before long our soldier finds two more occasions to prove himself right by acting out his winning computation. After two more sets of charges and two more trials, our once-decorated hero winds up in a penitentiary for most of his adult life. And while deprived of his freedom, our soldier whiles away his 20-year sentence, clinging to the certainty of how right he was to do what he had to do, and how wrong those who put him there were.

In many instances, people take on disabilities in order to survive. They receive sympathy when injured, so they come up with "survival" computations that include acting in a figuratively or actually injured manner in order to keep that sympathy coming. A person is not hassled and pushed to perform when he is ill, so he comes up with a computation that perpetuates that illness, or the general idea that it is best to become and remain ill when facing hassles.

There are no greater immediate gains observable from auditing than those attained on Grade 4. I have seen many people change their entire character for the better during Grade 4. I have seen many physical disabilities, including chronic aches and pains, disappear during Grade 4 auditing. I have heard preclears attest to greater depth of perception (including sight, smell, hearing, and tactile) during Grade 4. But what I have found most rewarding is consistently hearing preclears conclude that they are done with letting life run them; that they are going to strike out and develop their own potential and pursue worthwhile goals – which they for the most part do.

Now, here is the Black Dianetics corporate Scientology rub. Grade 4 auditing requires an alive, perceptive, and very competent auditor. Computations are so much a part of the individual that they are difficult to uncover. It requires a high degree of open communication on the part of auditor and preclear. Hubbard refers to all other auditing – that is, all auditing that is not Grade 4 auditing – as 'routine auditing,' in his injunction that Grade 4 handles that which 'routine auditing' does not address. Chapter 3 in this book, "Training," describes why corporate Scientologists are incapable of performing Grade 4 auditing. They are trained to be such perfect robots that the level of open, deeply searching communication required to unearth actual computations is rendered impossible. Rather than find and run out genuine computations at Grade 4, Scientology Inc. auditors find and run preclears' mundane, garden-variety thoughts and considerations. The actual, debilitating computations are left more firmly in place than ever.

Exacerbating the situation is the fact that in order to survive in the threatening environment that is corporate Scientology, it is necessary for Scientologists to develop computations, and nasty ones at that. As noted in our war hero example, a key element in the development of a computation is the inability to communicate about the survival problem one is facing. Recall our soldier: he came up with the computation "in order to survive I must fight to the death" when on the battlefield it was impossible to communicate about the life-threatening problem he was facing. As we noted in chapters 7, 8 and 9, a police state has arisen in corporate Scientology where all members must closely guard the ideas they might express, and even the thoughts that might form within their own minds. Within corporate Scientology culture, it is not safe to communicate about anything that is awry about Scientology. Further, Scientologists are continually being served up threats to their survival by the "church" they pay to keep in operation.

Say the wrong word, exhibit the wrong attitude, explore the Internet, read a forbidden newspaper or book, even be seen acting friendly toward someone who has done these things, and the next thing a corporate Scientologist could face is overnight conversion to non-person status. Thus, being strictly forbidden to examine or communicate about problems, the corporate Scientologist is forced to create aberrated evaluations and postulates (computations) to cope with survival in that culture. In this way, Scientology Inc. culture is the breeding ground for hundreds of computations along the following lines, every day:

"The best way to communicate with family is to be uncommunicative"

"To achieve an image of openness and honesty, one must be stealthy and dishonest"

"In order to attain social harmony, I need to be anti-social"

"To achieve enlightenment, I must remain in the dark"

And on and on they go. Crippling, self-generated life axioms, implanted and acted out, all seemingly pro-survival for corporate Scientology in the short term, all devastating for the individual and the group in the long run. Given the corporate Scientology auditor's strict training regimen, and close supervision of his auditing by the organizations, there is no chance any of these types of group-preserving computations would be touched with a ten foot pole, let alone audited out of the individual. It has become so reversed that former corporate Scientologists I have audited have uncovered computations that they formulated while in sessions on Grade-4-type auditing within Scientology Inc. The very process intended to free a person of computations is used to create them in corporate Scientology.

By auditing dozens of former members, by talking with hundreds of former members, and by closely watching and listening to Scientologists for 35 years, I have noted several computations that could be considered group-required ones within corporate Scientology. The most prevalent and most solidly ingrained one goes something like this: "Since the future of the planet is dependent upon the church's survival, I must be a warrior against its detractors." This one is really at the core, and after any extended involvement with corporate Scientology, an individual is required to add it to his mental baggage in order to carry on. All the reversed techniques of Scientology (read 'Black Dianetics') that we have covered thus far in this book are geared toward implanting that computation into the minds of corporate Scientologists.

Thus, we witness Tom Cruise lovingly referring to the sociopath to end all sociopaths, David Miscavige, as the greatest leader he has ever met – emphasizing his certainty by reminding his audience that he has met all world leaders.

Thus, virtually every day we witness families destroyed by parents forsaking their children, or children denouncing their parents, for harboring a thought that does not precisely align with the Scientology Inc. party line.

Thus, we see the corporation's dirty tricks department, Office of Special Affairs (OSA), utilizing any means necessary, fair or foul, to silence, censor and destroy critics of the machine.

At the core of all of this insanity is the implanted computation, "Since the future of the planet is dependent upon the church's survival, I must be a warrior against its detractors."

It would be extreme, and it would not be quite the whole truth, to characterize corporate Scientologists as the victims of a vast, diabolically effective and corrupt machine that has stolen their minds. They too hold responsibility for the condition we find them in. Somewhere along the line, each of them compromised his or her own integrity. To treat them otherwise would be to countenance their anti-social behaviors.

Eventually, they see the light only when the abuse they have tolerated and perpetuated becomes intolerable to them. It is their own personal integrity that decides, for each of them, where that point is reached. Each of them made a decision to forfeit his or her own personal integrity. Only after that were they rendered susceptible and agreeable to the rest of it. A good description of that decision point is found in *The Age of Reason* by Thomas Paine:

It is impossible to calculate the moral mischief, if I may so express it, that mental lying has produced in society. When a man has so far corrupted and prostituted the chastity of his mind, as to subscribe his professional belief to things he does not believe, he has prepared himself for the commission of every other crime.

Ultimately, an individual must come to grips with his own mental lying to himself. Anything that assists an individual – within the bounds of decency and the law – to recall and face that point is a valid remedy for the Scientology Inc. computation. Grade 4, effectively practiced as originally intended, can help in that process, as well as clear up the accumulated effects that the forfeiture of one's personal integrity has wrought.

CHAPTER ELEVEN

CLEAR

In many lectures and books that correspond to the Scientology Grades, Hubbard describes how each particular Grade alone could explain the construction and continued creation of the reactive mind by each individual.

On Academy training Level 0, one reads the book *Dianetics 55!*, which explains the creation of all of human aberration and suffering solely within the framework of violation of the laws of communication.

At Level 1, Hubbard speaks of the creation of mental mass and energy stemming from the mechanics of problems. That is, briefly, as one intention collides with a counter-intention, a persistence of energy (which, compacted sufficiently, becomes matter or mass) is created, which suspends in time.

Hubbard speaks at Level 2 of the Overt Act-Motivator sequence, where the process of a thetan holding on to his secrets suspends mental image pictures in time.

At Level 3, where upsets are addressed, as well as tolerance for and ability to effectuate change, we learn that resistance to change creates suspended energy and mass across time.

A review of Chapter 10 will demonstrate the potential for a person creating a reactive mind with only Grade 4 mechanics in play – his computations creating the stimulus-response characteristics of the reactive mind.

When a person completes Grades, the final step toward Clear – Dianetics engram running – becomes relatively easy. The individual is far more able to correlate and understand the mechanics of the reactive mind as he erases engrams through Dianetics procedure. Before long, the individual sees his own responsibility in the matter. This is occasioned by a sudden disappearance of all the stimulus-response machinery the fellow has been carrying around and enslaved by, since time immemorial.

Jason Beghe's coming-out video, which we touched on in the introduction to this book, contained some punchy one-liners that resonated with many former Scientologists and anti-Scientologists. One in particular involved the state of Clear. Jason bellowed challengingly, "Show me a mother-f******* Clear!" That has served as an oft-repeated mantra of critics who seem to make an occupation of attempting to discredit L. Ron Hubbard and Scientology. The burden of Jason's accompanying discourse was to question whether a state of Clear even existed or was attainable.

Jason implied that Hubbard was a con, based on his interpretation of a sequential study of Hubbard's lectures delivered throughout the '50s. He characterized Hubbard's modus operandi as defining what a Clear was, then lecturing and experimenting and announcing attainment of that state, then following up a year later with an admission, "Oh, we really didn't achieve that, but I've found the real route to Clear now," while redefining what attainment of Clear was. It was an interpretation that had never occurred to me before. I attempted to take Jason's viewpoint in order to see it. I kept that viewpoint in mind while I listened to all of Hubbard's 1950s lectures again. I attempted to make the fraud theory work, but in the end I could not.

The problem with the con theory is that Hubbard stated repeatedly during that development period that two factors were in continuous play. First, Hubbard always approached research and practice with goals in mind. He admittedly always aimed high. As Viktor Frankl (author of *Man's Search for Meaning*) so well explained in a filmed lecture he gave to students of psychology, in any mental or spiritual therapy the practitioner must always aim far, far beyond where he ultimately hopes to go. Life's suppressors can be likened to a constantly blowing gale from the north. Given that built-in resistance, if one sails from the west Atlantic shore at the equator and wants to arrive in North Africa, he had better keep his ship headed toward Europe most of the way. Second, the more spiritual practices that were attempted by application, the more Hubbard – and we – learned about the mind and spirit. What Hubbard described in 1950 in the book Dianetics was like cave drawings compared to what he had discovered about the spirit by the end of that decade. What Jason apparently took for con, I saw as continual sharing of research and result, every step of the way – good, bad, pretty or ugly.

Another factor ought to be kept in mind during any study of the entire track of Dianetics and Scientology research. That is, there is no evidence to suggest Hubbard was not achieving his stated idea of Clear with any number of people. Hubbard spent a tremendous amount of that research and development period improving the abilities of auditors, noting that a central problem he was trying to solve was how to empower others to obtain the results he was able to achieve as an auditor. He continuously aimed to make the results of the journey more routinely achievable by greater numbers of people. He was admittedly fine-tuning the path every day for the rest of his life. The track of his research, studied in chronological sequence, demonstrates that rather plainly.

As far as the end phenomenon reached or state attained at Clear is concerned, to an auditor trained to that level, there is absolutely no question when one sees it achieved. Despite all postulated characteristics that Hubbard targeted to achieve during the first eight years of his research, what constituted the state of Clear remained largely constant from 1958 forward. In July of that year, Hubbard, in his inimitable style, described the achievable qualities of Clear, from a number of different perspectives, in a series of several lectures entitled *The Clearing Congress*. One of those perspectives was the analogy of the valences (identity characteristics of others) we collect, forgetting where we got them from, and then unknowingly wear, masking our own basic personality. Hubbard likened those valences to jackets we wear – layer upon layer of them. What the auditor does is assist a fellow to remove the synthetic personality jackets, and when he's removed all that do not inherently belong to the preclear, the fellow recognizes his true self and has achieved Clear. He noted, "A thetan already has a basic personality, and this is what we are trying to uncover in Scientology in order to make a Clear. And it is as easy as that…a Clear could be said to be basic personality revealed."

When a preclear recognizes the source of the automatic, stimulus-response mental machinery that masks his basic, native spiritual personality, that machinery stops operating. The preclear recognizes his own self, without outside-influenced embellishments, and he becomes a self-determined, rational, spiritual, and reasonably happy person. Between 1958 and the mid-'60s, L. Ron Hubbard intensively worked with the route toward that goal – all well documented by near-daily lectures and bulletins issued during that period – culminating with the organized Bridge (Grades and Dianetics auditing leading to Clear) which we outlined in Chapter 1. During that period the definition or stated characteristics of what constituted the state of Clear did not change significantly.

Is Clear a permanent state? No. Hubbard made that plain in a 1978 bulletin to auditors and case supervisors responsible for determining whether or not a person has honestly achieved the state. In the bulletin he explained that a Clear was as capable as anyone else of creating mental machinery and automaticities to do his thinking for him, but that "practice increases his general reality." In other words, one must learn to walk the walk. One has been helped off his crutches and what he does, now that he is standing, is up to him. If he wants to use his increased intelligence and ability to fool, con, or entrap others, he will reap what he sows. If, instead, he wants to build on those capabilities and increase his awareness and reach, he will learn to walk, then to jog, then to trot, then to run. And who knows but that someday he won't fly? I do not know who determined not to show this bulletin to Clears, but I do know its withholding has caused a lot of heartache to the many who have been led to believe that the day they attest to the state of Clear and forever after, they are going to be a super-hero without even trying.

Where corporate Scientology specializes in reversing the process on Clears is in the first quality of the state of Clear that I noted above, self-determinism. This, I believe, is the critical turning point I alluded to Jason and me hitting, in this book's introduction: that point where the organization's focus shifted from freeing an individual, over to a reverse-vector effort to contain the individual. I must give the devil his due: Scientology Inc. is capable of producing the state of Clear. But before long it can be counted upon to snatch defeat from the jaws of victory by severely reducing an individual's newly-found self-determinism.

For example, for more than ten years, Miscavige has institutionalized the practice of selling and subjecting Clears and OTs (Operating Thetans, those who have engaged in Scientology levels above Clear) to dozens upon dozens of intensives (12½-hour blocks) of Objectives auditing. A quick review of Chapter 5, Objectives, would make plain to a non-Scientologist that no one in his or her right mind would work for years to achieve the state of Clear, and then spend a minor fortune for the privilege of learning the art of interminably executing meaningless orders. One must ask, "Why do they do it?"

The end phenomenon of the state of Clear has been defined and available since 1958, in the form of Hubbard's lecture series *The Clearing Congress*. Yet hundreds of veteran Clears have paid untold sums of money to be subjected to torturous auditing that sought to invalidate their attainment of that state, and created uncertainty about what constitutes Clear in the first place. One must ask, "Why do they do it?"

In 1978, when Hubbard did his final fine-tuning of Dianetics auditing techniques and had his final revisions packaged into a neat, organized series of bulletins detailing precisely how it was to be done, he also issued a bulletin labeled prominently at the top with the words "**Urgent – Important**." The bulletin was entitled ***DIANETICS FORBIDDEN ON CLEARS AND OTS*** (capital letters and boldface type in original). The bulletin hammered in a policy that virtually all Scientologists are aware of: it is strictly forbidden to apply Dianetics engram running type auditing on anyone who has achieved the state of Clear. In a number of other writings, Hubbard not only reiterated the injunction, he made clear there were no exceptions, and that the spiritual consequences of violating that policy would be devastating to the recipient. Now, in the light of this well-known Scientology law, David Miscavige has subjected hundreds, if not thousands, of Clears to many intensives of Dianetics auditing. The validity of Hubbard's warning about the undesirable effect of said practice has been witnessed by me in several of Miscavige's victims who have left Scientology Inc. and sought succor in our home. Yet hundreds more continue to create precarious financial situations for themselves, in order to continue to subject themselves to Miscavige's Dianetics-auditing-on-Clears version of Black Dianetics. One must ask, "Why do they do it?"

Having dealt with dozens of casualties of Miscavige's Black Dianetics assault on Clears and OTs, the answer is much the same for each: They never even considered the question, "Do I go with Ron Hubbard's technology, or do I submit to David Miscavige's?" Instead, they never drew a distinction between Ron Hubbard and David Miscavige in the first place. They placed their faith in the leadership of Scientology Inc. They did so, in part, because L. Ron Hubbard told them to do so time and again in many policy directives spanning over decades. It resulted in Scientologists failing to see the difference between the philosophy and the organization. Therein lies the crux of the organization's power to practice Black Dianetics wholesale. The road to recovery begins with the differentiation of L. Ron Hubbard from David Miscavige.

CHAPTER TWELVE

DIFFERENTIATION

Virtually everyone whom I have met who knew L. Ron Hubbard personally described him in words to the effect of "larger than life." That comes from a wide spectrum of people, from those who loved him to those who sharply criticized him. I never met him, and in a way I am glad I did not. To me, the ultimate worth of what he created can only be measured against the standard of whether what he wrote and lectured about can produce desirable effects or not. In the end, that is how he wished it to be. He noted in one of his final journals to Scientologists that his legacy would be the technology he would leave behind – not his personality, not his biography, not his recognitions and awards, not any God-like abilities that others must continue to create in their minds and rely upon, and not his frailties and shortcomings.

It was Hubbard's charismatic and infectious personality that led critics back in the '80s to predict that Scientology would die once he passed away. Some have since claimed that Hubbard's January, 1986 death did indeed mark the beginning of the end of Scientology. While both of these assertions were close to the mark, in my view they were not quite accurate in a couple of respects. First, a semantics note. True, the church of Scientology is dead, for all intents and purposes. But that is an organization, a corporate conglomerate. Scientology itself is a religious philosophy, and that has not died. A philosophy cannot be killed, any more than an idea can be extinguished. True, the church of Scientology began to die after its founder's demise. However, the passing of Hubbard did not kill it. Instead, during the confusion and pain of Scientologists' mourning Hubbard's death, a deadly virus was stealthily injected into Scientology culture.

That virus was a falsehood. The church of Scientology began its death slide when its leaders declared Hubbard had not really died. They asserted that Hubbard intentionally left the flesh so as to better research and monitor that which he had created. They did not outright state it, but the bold-faced, bald-faced sub-text was "Hubbard is God."

The religion or philosophy of Scientology had done well during Hubbard's lifetime. That was partly due to the fact that when he was around, he wouldn't stand for lounging in the comfort of being considered a deity. Even though some of his writings could be construed to mean Hubbard thought of himself as a special breed of being who visited this planet to free the imprisoned mortals, in practice he was largely content living out the life of a prophet and not a God.

Hubbard, like so many larger-than-life Americans before him, wittingly or not, played out the Moses story. Bruce Fielder's *Moses: America's Prophet*, detailed how political figures throughout American history, from George Washington to Barack Obama, had invoked Moses' life story. From the left in Franklin Delano Roosevelt, to the right in Ronald Reagan – Moses's good name was used to describe leaders in America. The life of Moses was used as script throughout America's struggle for civil rights, from Old John Brown at Harper's Ferry to Martin Luther King in Memphis. They took on the determined visage of Moses, selflessly leading people toward the promised land, even though prohibited by God himself from making it there themselves.

While sacrificing one's life for the benefit of others was the central theme of this oft-repeated passion play, there was and is a big difference between a Jesus (as personification of God) type sacrifice, and one of the Moses (a prophet) variety. A prophet does his work as a man and leaves this world as a man. He lives a remarkable story, inspiring many along the way. But when the clay deteriorates, the spirit moves on and the only legacy left behind is the man's work.

Jesus, on the other hand, was elevated to the position of the Son of God after he passed on, and as such never really left. Whether he had a say in that holy status is still the subject of hot debate. Not too long ago, an agnostic friend of mine in South Texas told me about a Christian retreat he planned to attend. According to him, it was often frequented by a group of fellow intellectuals and scholars.

I asked, "Why would an agnostic go to a Christian retreat?" He replied, "Because I respect the work of Jesus. This group has done a lot of historical study and believes that Christian worshipers can't fully appreciate the lessons of Jesus's life because they mistakenly consider him God."

He explained that one little mistranslated line from Jesus (a la John Steinbeck's *East of Eden*) started 2,000 years of misunderstanding, ignorance, intolerance, inquisitions and wars. During Jesus's Roman trial, magistrate Pontius Pilate asked him the all-important question, "Do you contend that you are the son of God?" Worshippers are taught that Jesus replied, "Yes, I am the son of God." This group of

Texas agnostics claims the answer in fact was, "Yes, we are all the children of God."

Whether that matter of mistranslation is historically accurate or not, the contention of these fellows is that once a teacher, a prophet, or messiah is anointed with deity status, the burden or responsibility of conduct and understanding and enlightenment shifts from the individual to the deity. In the case of Jesus, his lessons do not simply stand alone on their own merit anymore. They must be adhered to as a matter of belief, rather than adopted after critical examination and practice to determine worth. The merits of an individual and his salvation are no longer dependent upon how he conducts his life, as much as his willingness to surrender and devote himself unconditionally to the will of a God. And by that leap of faith, the believer's own responsibility and judgment are forfeited. Given the invisibility of the ultimate Judge, that leap then opens the door for priests, institutions, organizations and churches to profit from their supposed superior understandings of God, or convincing displays that they can somehow enhance the communication lines to and from God. As Thomas Paine competently demonstrated more than 200 years ago in *The Age of Reason*, this via-to-God business has for centuries been used very effectively to keep the masses ignorant, violent and effectively in a state of slavery, all the while lining the pockets of the self-appointed messengers.

Whether one buys into the semantics/mistranslation story or Paine's theory about the effect of greedy manipulators corrupting religions from their inceptions, those who know a little about Scientology can appreciate the relevance of both to what happened with Hubbard and his church. Hubbard made it a strict policy that Scientology study must begin with a course on how to study. That course emphasizes that one should study Scientology with a critical mind, and continually apply the standard that Hubbard's words are not true for an individual until that person actually witnesses that those words produce the intended result.

Hubbard wrote many times that he was merely a man, and spoke in several recorded lectures of the dangers of appointing higher authorities (real or imagined) to whom one transfers responsibility for determining one's destiny.

And so, quite the sleight-of-hand was accomplished in the last week of January, 1986 when a couple of self-styled "young Turks" pulled the wool over thousands of Scientologists' eyes. Pat Broeker and David Miscavige had seized joint power over Hubbard's kingdom, by virtue of their gatekeeper positions during the last five years of Hubbard's life. Living in seclusion and wishing the utmost in security, Hubbard had been well served by Broeker and Miscavige on that score. Broeker in his early 30s, and Miscavige in his early 20s, were energetic masters of the cloak-and-dagger game such uber-security required. However, Hubbard's trust of intelligence acumen over understanding and mastery of the philosophy he had created ultimately betrayed his better intentions.

Of primary concern to Miscavige and Broeker was whether Scientologists would follow their lead, as the group had followed Hubbard's for thirty-six years. They also happened to share another attitude that they successfully withheld from other Scientologists: joy that Hubbard's hands had let loose the reins of the Scientology empire and the thrill of the prospect of sitting in the throne of unquestioned power.

Steve "Sarge" Pfauth, a trusted associate and friend to Hubbard to the end, described the Miscavige/Broeker chemistry the day after Hubbard died: "The day after I witnessed [Hubbard's] death certificate, Miscavige and Broeker were sitting in the living room, laughing and joking. Miscavige was like a little kid; he was bouncing around like nothing happened. They were laughing and planning and joking. I cried the whole day. So did Annie." (Annie was the late Ann Tidman Broeker, Pat Broeker's then-wife and Hubbard's closest aide.)

Hubbard's body was not yet cold or stiff before Broeker and Miscavige began plotting consolidation of power for Scientology's second generation. How would they convince thousands of veteran Scientologists across the world to follow them? Those thousands revered a man who had beaten all odds to create and expand a non-conformist spiritual movement in the heart of intolerant Cold War America. How would Broeker and Miscavige convince them to follow a couple of brash young guns who had only perfected the darker arts of public relations and espionage? They solved the problem by exploiting their best shared trait, chutzpah. Borrowing a page out of the Nazi propaganda playbook, they came up with a carefully orchestrated big lie. They would capitalize on Scientologists' abiding respect and love for Hubbard and his philosophy. They would play on the collective grief of Scientology followers losing their leader. They would shock and awe the emotionally weakened Scientology masses into line by introducing L. Ron Hubbard as God. It was biblical in significance, right on down to creating what would become a Hubbard resurrection myth.

And it took. Before long, though, Broeker paid the price of dealing with the devil. Within three years, Miscavige had carefully orchestrated his demise from leadership, purging him from the corporate Scientology ranks. The price all Scientologists paid for checking their intelligence at the door would be crippling. An angry young man with a Napoleonic complex, Miscavige would be elevated to somewhere between mere mortal and Hubbard's God-like status. He would become the monopoly holder on the communication channel to God; one of the high priests Tom Paine warned us about in *Age of Reason*.

Miscavige would create a position of authority over Scientologists that L. Ron Hubbard would not even permit for himself during his life. Hubbard would not permit it because it was anathema to the very logic Scientology was predicated upon. The moment a "God" appeared, an individual turned over the controls of his own determinism to an outside agency. To do so, Hubbard commented many times and in many ways, would be tantamount to forfeiting one's power of reason, responsibility, and destiny.

To make matters worse, the self-appointed demigod does not and never did understand Scientology. Whereas most people approached the subject with the purpose of increasing spiritual awareness and helping others, Miscavige came in with a completely different set of motivations. He wanted to become powerful, not so much to attain the aims of Scientology as to punish a world that he apparently considered had dealt him an unfair hand, and mistreated him as a sickly child. Over the next quarter century, the organizations, their staff, and their followers would increasingly be molded into the image of their leader. An organization that once stood for non-conformity, thinking outside the box, freedom of conscience, freedom of information and nurturing of the spiritual would degenerate into a mind-controlling, intolerant, censoring, zealous, violent and materialistic cult.

Many bitter, former Scientologists and devoted critics of Scientology and Hubbard have chafed at the notion that Miscavige could have so effectively betrayed the intentions and will of such a powerful and driven man as Hubbard. There is a germ of truth in that kernel. It will take the future, larger history volume I have referred to, to unravel that complex web. But for the purposes of our discussion here, please note that I peg the first, fundamental betrayal as occurring after L. Ron Hubbard died. Even if the world knew that Miscavige was nothing but a mere messenger boy who had ruthlessly clawed his way to the top of an organization in crisis, the damage he has wrought through his original sin is fairly irreversible in corporate Scientology. As we shall see, positioning L. Ron Hubbard as God in the eyes of Scientologists has effectively converted Scientology into an elaborate trap.

CHAPTER THIRTEEN

REVERSAL

Miscavige's elevation of L. Ron Hubbard to God-like status, and himself to demigod status, has provided Miscavige with carte-blanche to reverse the entire vector of Scientology's aims and activities.

He began by perpetrating a fraud upon the highest-level Scientologists, Clears and OTs, with his promise of upper OT Levels allegedly in his possession. While the seed was planted at the January 1986 funeral event, it has been a cleverly-played mind game on Scientologists ever since. Miscavige has devoted most of his attention to keeping these highest-level Scientologists on the farm for a reason. He knows that they are the opinion leaders among the general membership. With the opinion leaders doing his bidding, he is able to keep the majority of his followers in the dark. At this he has done a masterful job. But to ascribe any great virtue or power to him for having done so would be a mistake. Without L. Ron Hubbard, David Miscavige would be little more than a clever, overly-aggressive con man. To pretend that Miscavige perfected his consolidation of power without the help of Hubbard's own decisions and policy would be naïve and untrue. In fact, to so pretend would require quite an invalidation of Hubbard's abilities, and the power of the technology he discovered.

Without the backing of Hubbard-authored Scientology policy, David Miscavige could never have created the Black Dianetics monopoly Hubbard had warned against many years before. How could such a contradiction be possible? That is a complicated story. For purposes of our discussion here, I will provide a brief summation of what will be more fully treated in a later volume.

In short, human beings are full of contradictions, and L. Ron Hubbard was not immune from that imperfection. For better or for worse, during the '60s, when Hubbard and Scientology were continually facing attacks intended to bring about their demise, Hubbard issued quite a bit of policy in response which changed the character of the movement. This "wartime" left an indelible imprint on Scientology. It was a dark ages of sorts for the movement. It was a time when the group, as a matter of survival, needed to circle the wagons and know who was with it and who was against it. This was the era when security checks became routine. This was the period when 'disconnection' from suppressive persons was dictated and enforced by the organizations. This was when policy called for the overt and covert destruction of alleged forces of evil. This was the period when Hubbard created a monster to achieve that end – an ogre that would later play an important role in his own demise. That was the Guardian's Office – a legal and public relations organization with its own intelligence network.

The Guardian's Office's intelligence system was once described by a government official in the know as rivaling that of Israel's state intelligence service (the storied Mossad). Hubbard wrote volumes of material for the Guardian's Office on how to smash and obliterate the "enemy." David Miscavige seized on this material during the early '80s, when the collective crimes of a decade and a half of unfettered Guardian's Office operations had come back to haunt Hubbard. Miscavige would rise, live and die by that wartime policy.

Miscavige became sort of a reactive mind of the Scientology machine. Just as the reactive mind drives all of the past into the present to haunt and torture the individual, Miscavige drove all of Hubbard's "war" era policy to the present, to haunt and torture Scientologists – and Scientology's detractors – from the '80s forward.

The way in which Miscavige corralled Clears and OTs, however, begins with a seemingly benign policy. That is a Hubbard policy letter of 1967, entitled *An Open Letter to All Clears*. It is the first thing a newly-arrived Clear is required to read.

Hubbard represented consistently and repeatedly, from 1950 to the mid-'60s, that the quest for Clear is the pursuit of personal freedom and personal confidence, to the point of self-trust and being worthy of trust by one's peers. In the face of that continual statement of purpose and goal, the *Open Letter* begins hedging on those representations. It begins indoctrinating the Clear into the idea that whatever sacrifices the individual might have made to achieve the state of Clear, the ledger of responsibility is not balanced. The Clear has obligations to Hubbard and Scientology, and is expected to comply with group directives in order to pay off the debt, particularly if one should wish to rise to greater heights than Clear. The Clear is told, in *Open Letter*:

An ethical code already exists for OTs so at the state of Clear one should not assume that one has a license to do just whatever one will...

...So, the policies of Scientology which have enabled you to reach the state of Clear still apply to all Clears. In fact, they apply more because you have the reality of their value and the necessity of seeing that they are followed...

...As a result, bigger responsibilities will be given and expected of you so you must be prepared to responsibly educate yourself where necessary so that you can do whatever is assigned to you in a proper manner, in keeping with the main goals and aims of Scientology....

...It is a crime to invalidate the state of Clear – see to it that you don't do this in your conduct as a Clear, particularly as regards yourself....

...You have now become more than ever a part of a team. Obsessive individualism and a failure to organize were responsible for our getting into the state we got into....

...As soon as you have gone the rest of the way this will become abundantly plain....

...I expect and need your help to carry out the broad mission of decontaminating this area of the universe....

And so, the promise of a Golden Age of reason among free-thinking, un-policed Clears was replaced with the news that the organizations would be enforcing your duty to follow an "ethical code" and the "policies of Scientology." It announces that you will comply with "whatever is assigned to you" by the organization. Should any Clear bristle at this news, it is quickly pointed out that he is simply dramatizing the "obsessive individualism" that was "responsible for our getting into the state we got into." For my part, the most empowering cognition I came to in my own travels along the Bridge was that I no longer had to agree with anyone. I no longer felt compelled to go along with group-think. This was the key to breaking the controlling, conforming conditioning that society tends to coerce us into accepting, including all the group thought patterns that justify greed, cheating, conflict and war. Upon indoctrination to *An Open Letter to All Clears*, I had to begin rationalizing, and thus invalidating, that new-found ability to chart my own course in life.

Thus, with *Open Letter*, and the volumes of policy it mandates now must be followed even more vigilantly, the vector became reversed. The door was opened to the evolution of an obsessive group devotion that graduated into the Big Brother corporation which went on to ruin the lives of thousands, and to lose whatever magic Dianetics and Scientology were capable of producing in the first place. It was bolstered by encyclopedic volumes of Scientology organizational policy. Most of that policy is very heady and workable material. It cannot be denied, however, that it is liberally spiked with a number of policies grooving in the idea that the group, the Scientology organization, is all important, and that its hierarchical structure must be respected and complied to, irrespective of who runs it.

Here is where the perversion we covered in Chapter 8, Ethics, receives its most potent authority. The overweighted third dynamic (group) would forever after skew the contemplation of the 'greatest good for the greatest number of dynamics' formula.

To gainsay this reality would be an exercise in denialism. For example, any Scientologist reading this book is automatically guilty of a variety of Scientology crimes and high crimes, by the mere act of reading. Per long-standing and currently-extant Hubbard Scientology policy, anyone who has read this far ought to be declared a suppressive person (a sociopath that both Hubbard and mental health authorities agree should be quarantined from society, without civil or constitutional rights). This is how Scientology organizational policy protects and perpetuates the vicious cult Miscavige has created.

Exacerbating matters is the fact that the first thing a Scientology Inc. Clear will encounter upon reaching that state is unrelenting pressure to get onto the Operating Thetan, or OT, levels. If a Clear wants to get on with life, exercise his new-found abilities and awareness so as to "practice to increase general reality" (as it was earlier noted that Hubbard had recommended) and resists compliance,

Scientology Inc. resorts to scare tactics. *An Open Letter to All Clears* is the first weapon in the organization's arsenal on that score. That is then compounded with the ultimate weapon, Hubbard's pronouncement that a Clear is at grave risk as a being if he or she does not get through the OT Levels as soon as possible. Ironically, that warning perhaps serves as the greatest invalidation of the state of Clear, which the *Open Letter* policy announces shall be considered a crime in itself.

As shall be made clear in the next chapter on the OT Levels, I am a huge proponent of the idea that the OT Levels are indeed capable of taking people to spiritual heights they never imagined possible. However, to ignore the shift of focus and the reversal-of-motivation tactic employed – even by Hubbard himself – would be to check my logic and personal integrity at the door. Just why Hubbard deviated from a 15-year devotion to creating a path that would only work where the practitioner's motivations were solely the pursuit of truth toward the empowerment of each individual addressed, into scare tactics aimed at having each individual surrender his or her self-determinism to the will of the group, is a complex matter. Warranted or not, much of what Hubbard and Scientology were facing in terms of opposition by vested interests by the mid-'60s wove its way into Hubbard's outlook, his thinking, and his overriding, strong intention that Scientology survive and be made available to humanity.

At bottom, it was Hubbard's reaction to what I consider ill-motivated, unethical, and vicious efforts by certain vested interests to keep him from achieving what he aimed for. Whether the response was an over-reaction or was necessary at that time is a question requiring a more in-depth history. For our purposes here – outlining what is wrong with Scientology – it is only necessary to highlight the contradictions that are obvious. Recognition of those contradictions makes patent the simple fact that to take every word Hubbard wrote literally, and treat it as commandment, puts one on a slippery, untenable slope. To do so would be just as irrational as criticizing and rejecting all of Hubbard's work and discoveries just because it is recognized he was not infallible. Exercising either extreme would be to employ the type of associative-reactive thought patterns his discoveries help people to overcome.

The problem with Hubbard's reaction to the attacks, and the ultimate product of that reaction, is that it puts an individual or group right back into that which they had sought to transcend through Scientology in the first place. Technically, it is a violation of one of his own fundamental maxims, "that which you resist, you become." It is perhaps best explained in Hubbard's own words, in the very lecture series, the 1958 *Clearing Congress*, where he finally settled on the parameters and qualities of Clear:

We get this sort of a situation where everybody's idea of everybody else becomes himself. Well, let's look at that. Here's Mr. A. Mr. A is certain that everybody around him is very evil and that they are "gonna get him" one way or the other. Now, Mr. A. has no choice – if he is also saddled with super-agreements, obsessive agreement, making equality a necessity – but to be this way himself.

Now, we ask this question: Does this evil character actually exist? And that's one of the first things we have to ask in clearing. Does this evil character exist?

It seems like we have a synthetic personality in existence which isn't really anybody, but is simply everybody's idea of how bad the other fellow is. This is pretty complicated, see. See, he's got the idea that this other fellow is so bad that he cannot help but criticize him violently. But because he is equal to this fellow over here, then, of course, he himself has to assume these characteristics of superlative evil. You see that? We get generals, admirals, politicians, all sorts of people, who have an idea that the enemy is so bad, or that the fellow man is so bad, or something else is so bad, they can't possibly live with it, and have therefore got to cut it to pieces. It's a very tricky thing. This has a vast bearing on clearing.

They've got to cut this evil being to pieces. Yes, but at the same time, they have an equality complex. By communicating with him, they therefore go into agreement with his evil characteristics, and the only thing they have left is an evil, synthetic personality which they themselves have to wear to be like everybody else and to be normal. This is one of the simplest and easiest tricks that is played in a culture.

So, what are you trying to do when you're clearing people? You've got to find the fellow himself and you also, as you go up the line – not an attribute of Clear, but an attribute of OT – have to give him a certainty on the other fellow.

Therein Hubbard echoed the ancient book of wisdom he once noted that much of Scientology had grown out of, *Tao Te Ching*, by Lao Tzu:

There is no greater misfortune than underestimating your enemy. Underestimating your enemy means thinking that he is evil. Thus you destroy your three treasures (simplicity, patience, compassion) and become an enemy yourself.

In the same 1958 lecture, Hubbard continued by warning against the temptation to create policing agencies:

…Well, all you'd have to do is have a police force and a society would start caving in. Why? The police force constitutes a constant reminder that men are evil, which is a constant reminder that we must agree with these evil men. Do you see how this would work? Neat little trick.

Now, that doesn't say that we are so starry-eyed as to believe that at this time we could dispense with all police. Or could we?

Now, you have to make up your mind which way you're going to go with a society, if you're thinking about a new society of one kind or another. And if you say, "Well, this society would be totally unregulated," then we would be proposing an anarchy. And all the anarchists tell us that the only way a society would work as a total freedom without government would be if everyone in it were perfect.

Well, I don't know whether we propose — when we talk about a cleared society — whether we propose or not to have an anarchy. That's beside the point. That's up to the people who get cleared. But I don't think you'd wind up with an anarchy. I think you'd wind up with a much finer level of agreement and cooperation, because I think you'd then be able to realize the rest of the dynamics.

Again, Hubbard was in perfect alignment with the Tao:

Throw away morality and justice, and people will do the right thing... The more prohibitions you have, the less virtuous the people will be... I let go of the law, and people become honest.

However, with the advent of tomes of policy, creating layers of hierarchical restriction upon the group and aggressive policing of its individuals' morals, the promise of the sanity and happiness of a cleared group and society was replaced. The new doctrinal paradigm held, in essence, that the only way to achieve a 'cleared society' was through a tightly-controlled, disciplined group whose survival trumped all other possible considerations. While volumes were written on how to run a Scientology organization in keeping with the goals of Clearing and the promise of OT, no matter how one dressed it up, Scientology policy created and required a force that one would have to be in utter denial to characterize as anything other than the *police* enforcing *prohibitions*, so as to protect good people from other people presumably dedicated to *evil*.

I am quite aware that these views will be condemned by many Scientologists, corporate and independent alike. But

I believe that if one dispassionately examines the facts of how Clears and OTs have come to be treated, how they have docilely accepted such treatment, and how they have come to behave within Scientology Inc., to ignore or deny Hubbard's empowerment of such treatment and behavior is tantamount to condemning Scientologists to repeating a history they are systemically required to remain ignorant of and yet perpetuate.

I am not contending that Hubbard was wrong to react to opposition in the way he did. Nor am I contending that he should not have memorialized his reaction under the heading of 'policy.' I do contend that to take Hubbard's policy literally, out of the time and the context in which it was born, is to become an extremist. With extremism comes the loss of the potential benefits that would otherwise accrue from application of the discoveries Hubbard made. In my opinion, nowhere is literalism and extremism more destructive than at the highest reaches of the Bridge, the OT levels.

CHAPTER FOURTEEN

OT LEVELS

About the only thing the world at large has been told about the OT Levels of Scientology is a science-fiction-like story which critics and media refer to as Scientology's 'creation myth.' As noted in Chapter 1, that is simply not the Scientology creation story. However, the harder the church denies the particulars of the leaked, confidential Hubbard OT Level writings from which this notion originates, the more solidly it seems to be cemented in the mind of the public. In short, the story goes that roughly 75 million years ago, thetans were transported to Earth and put through a nuclear holocaust incident in which they were grafted together with thousands of other thetans. A large part of OT Level auditing is the process of the individual auditing those entrapped thetans so as to free them, and free himself from their effects.

Bizarre, right? Just as surreal, I suppose, as any number of stories in the Bible, the Koran, and Eastern religious texts. L. Ron Hubbard acknowledged Greek philosophers, Jesus (and particularly accounts of him in the Bible's book of St. Luke), and the Buddha as sources consulted in the development of Scientology. Let us take these sources – who more people on earth acknowledge as credible sources than do not – one by one.

Greek philosophers – including Socrates and Plato – held to the notion that bodiless, spiritual entities exist and have an effect on the human psyche. They called them something roughly translatable to the English 'demons.' As far as Jesus goes, St. Luke portrays Christ's primary and most consistent practice as that of casting out demons from afflicted individuals. Some of the earliest, and thus most credible, accounts of Siddhartha Gautama's (the Buddha) quest for enlightenment portray the culmination of his spiritual journey seated at the foot of a tree. Gautama quieted himself, concentrated, and "faced down Mara and her armies." Mara and her armies were depicted as disembodied spiritual beings, invisible to the unenlightened eye. And when Buddha simply saw the truth of their existence, they disappeared – no longer affecting his being. Thus he achieved unfettered awareness and perception of the true nature of the universe and freedom from the endless cycle of birth and death.

To fixate on Gautama's Mara-and-her-armies construct, Jesus's agents-of-Satan construct, or Hubbard's space-opera construct would be to miss the forest for the trees. Even modern philosophers and secular theorists – having the advantage of decades of science coming closer to and acknowledging the effect of the spirit on the physical universe – have gravitated toward creating more "rational" constructs to explore the inexplicable. Thus, Ken Wilber, in *A Brief History of Everything*, postulates our creation of encysted globules of spirit which we carry along with us, and which persist until we face them and communicate with them. Then there is the modern and decidedly humanistic meme theory, creating a genetic-being-like embodiment to ideas that spread and persist among people. Whatever construct is used to describe the phenomenon, it seems that Christians, Buddhists, Hindus, philosophers – ancient and modern – and even humanists can agree on one thing: The invisible-to-the-eye spiritual phenomenon addressed by the Scientology OT Levels does exist, even if by another name or construct.

Partly because Hubbard initially communicated his construct in no uncertain terms as being historical fact, complications have arisen. I personally did not take Hubbard's colorful construct too literally when I was introduced to it. Unfortunately, corporate Scientologists take everything Hubbard wrote or stated literally. They are trained and coerced into doing so. As journalist Janet Reitman so astutely pointed out in her book *Inside Scientology*, that literalism makes corporate Scientologists much akin to fundamentalist religionists, irrationality and extremism included. Because of the good-vs.-evil, God-vs.-the Devil slant of the story, it seems that the higher up the Bridge Scientologists go, the more combative and insular they can become. Look at the cover of this book for but one example. The two bearded fellows dressed as space invaders – head cams and all – are leading corporate Scientology OTs. They are on my front doorstep demanding to enter my home, while announcing that this is a "bust" of a Scientology heretic. They continued in such fashion for 199 days, despite drawing continual international media attention for their bizarre harassment tactics. Thus it is no wonder that the public at large carries some anxious notions as to the safety and sanity of pursuing the higher levels of Scientology. High level members behave as if the end times are near, and treat detractors as if the latter were some sort of alien adversaries, potentially disrupting the entire galactic cosmos.

I am of the opinion that in his later years, L. Ron Hubbard recognized that characterizing his OT Levels story as historical fact was a mistake. Just a couple of years before his death, Hubbard wrote to the highest technical official within Scientology Inc., noting that the particular level where the story is studied may well be superfluous. In 1978, he had developed far more direct processes for dealing with the phenomena addressed at that level.

Hubbard ordered that a pilot program be implemented where Clears who were just beginning the OT Levels skip OT 3 – where the space opera story appears – and instead go directly onto the following level, which makes no reference to OT 3 in theory or procedure. However, David Miscavige – who ran all matters on the ground at the international headquarters by then – had other priorities, and the pilot program Hubbard ordered was never attempted, before or after his death.

Perhaps Miscavige's motivation for never completing the ordered pilot program is answered by his desire to maintain a 'creation myth.' As Tom Paine argues in *Age of Reason*, creation stories have historically served one common, continuous purpose: to manipulate and control populations. As long as Miscavige has his veteran, leading members convinced, as a matter of strongly-held belief, that any criticism or opposition to his own authority is motivated by the agents of darkness, as memorialized in the OT 3 story, he keeps them from questioning him – and instead has them attempting to burn heretics like me, or entire classes of people such as psychiatrists and psychologists. In either event, corporate Scientology's vehement refusal to acknowledge the story only increases the mystery of its alleged power. The organization's increasingly extremist end-times-like behavior makes all the more credible the allegation that it maintains a mysterious, confidential creation story. More importantly, corporate Scientologists' adherence to such strongly-held beliefs defeats the entire purpose the subject was created to achieve.

Whether I am right or wrong about how Hubbard ultimately conceptualized the phenomena dealt with on the OT Levels, I believe the space-opera story is a result of two very common human tendencies. The first is our habit of anthropomorphization. That is the practice of ascribing human-form characteristics to observed phenomena. We all do that. It creates a familiar construct by which to better understand unfamiliar phenomena.

Nothing wrong with it, except when we take the anthropomorphizing constructs too seriously. The second is our love of the narrative. As Nassim Nicholas Taleb covered in his bestseller *The Black Swan*, humans tend to teach, learn, and think in terms of stories. The narrative is humankind's most-utilized method of creating constructs. But Taleb noted that it is so ingrained that it can serve as the greatest barrier to conceptual, abstract thinking. When we think only in terms of narratives, or take them too literally, we limit our intellectual capabilities.

Excessive anthropomorphizing and storytelling – or taking them too seriously or literally – calls to mind the ancient Zen Buddhist parable (a story-telling anthropomorphization in itself), about the student who is blinded by awe of his teacher: The student who never sees the moon is the one who remains too focused on the master's hand pointing to it.

Ironically, it was Hubbard's description of similar pitfalls of science that intensely interested me in Scientology in the first place. Not anthropomorphizing and narratives, but their cousin, the creation of constructs. Hubbard noted in lectures I listened to that the thetan, not being of the physical universe, was denied by science since science was only capable of measuring or perceiving, with the traditional five senses, things of the physical universe. Accepted scientific constructs were limited by the disallowance of the imperceptible (by science) creator of that which they were exploring (matter, energy, space and time). That was very real to me, having just spent two years in college trying to wrap my wits around biology and physics and sensing something awfully fundamental missing from the picture the traditional subjects painted.

In my experience, rationally practiced, the OT levels heighten perception and awareness of that creating life force, the spirit or the thetan. On the OT Levels, an individual learns to solo audit. Solo auditing is, in essence, the process of the individual extending his attention and intention across space from himself, to communicate with phenomena in his environment (imperceptible by the traditional five senses) – phenomena which register on an E-meter. Whatever construct one wishes to use in order to describe the phenomena the solo auditor so addresses is of little import. What is of greater importance is that the solo auditor finds that through practice he can perceive, reach by intention, and communicate telepathically across distance. By extensive practice and processes, the solo auditor's theta perceptions (sixth sense and beyond) are discovered and improved. The solo auditor who stays with it begins to experience perceptions and abilities in what he discovers is a universe distinct from the physical – the spiritual or theta universe. The theta universe contains no matter, energy, space or time as we commonly know such. If the solo auditor keeps at it, he increases his ability to communicate and convey intention telepathically to others, and to perceive intention and non-verbal communication from others as well. If one moves up from Clear, in the manner I earlier noted Hubbard advised – by 'practice increases general reality' in life – he will see with greater regularity that what is occurring in the solo auditing session extends to his perceptions and abilities in life.

After much practice, my subjective experience has been to gain the ability to routinely observe the creation of matter, energy, space and time by theta. By practicing in life, and not simply treating solo auditing as some therapy fix, I am able to cease unwittingly continuing to create the physical. I am also increasingly more able to effortlessly cause life to take the path I choose. I am more frequently able to telepathically communicate with others over greater distances. In short, I believe solo auditing has helped me to achieve greater clarity of perception and lightness and dexterity of spirit.

By now, I am sure that critics, humanists, atheists, former Scientologists and even spiritualists and practitioners of other faiths are likely guffawing or sneering. That is understandable. I will be the first to admit that all I have related is purely subjective. But this is my book, and I am communicating through it my reality as best I know how. I don't expect it to be believed, adopted, or accepted. I merely proffer it as my experience.

Oddly enough, science may ultimately afford the best validation of what I have communicated. With increasing frequency, accomplished and recognized scientists are postulating that the physical universe is created by the spirit, or consciousness, and not the other way around. The trend is occasioned by a number of scientific experiments that have concluded that at sub-atomic particle or wave level, the observer of phenomena (the being, or thetan) affects the manner in which particles or waves behave.

Many of these scientists continue to be confused in their attempts at defining the observer – alternately calling it 'brain,' 'mind,' 'consciousness' or 'spirit.' But they are right there measuring life force indirectly by noting whatever-it-is's effect on the physical universe. Of course the source of the confusion is that the thetan itself cannot be directly measured with physical-universe tools, since it is not of the physical universe – just as Hubbard noted in defining 'thetan' as "…having no mass, no wave-length, no energy and no time or location in space except by consideration or postulate. The spirit is not a thing. It is the creator of things."

Hubbard's axioms, covered in Chapter 1, no longer seem so "out there" to those at the cutting edge of quantum physics and biology. Astrophysicist Bernard Haisch posits, in his 2006 book, *The God Theory*: "I am proposing…that ultimately it is consciousness that is the origin of matter, energy, and the laws of nature in this universe and all others that may exist." Leading advanced cell technologist Robert Lanza has created an entirely new subject, *Biocentrism*, to explore more deeply the role of consciousness (read 'the spirit') in the creation of the physical universe. For those still wishing to pigeon-hole Hubbard as nothing more than a science fiction writer with a vivid imagination, consider that Lanza wrote a chapter in his first book on biocentrism, entitled "Sci-Fi Gets Real." There he credits the rise in popularity of science fiction as opening scientific consciousness to the possibility of understanding invisible life force.

Scott Tyson, another leading scientist exploring consciousness's seniority to the physical universe, in *The Unobservable Universe* credited the rising popularity of Eastern spiritualism as opening the door to his discoveries. No one with more experience in the fields of science fiction, Eastern thought, and western practicality has approached the field of mind over matter than L. Ron Hubbard. Haisch, Tyson and Lanza are only three of many leading scientific minds now grappling with the idea – and running into evidence to suggest it – that mind really does take precedence over matter, or that spirit does transcend the physical, and perhaps even creates it. Perhaps the best work on the convergence of science and spirituality has been produced by Lynne McTaggart, see *The Field* and *The Intention Experiment*.

I am not recommending this line of study to try to prove that L. Ron Hubbard was ahead of his time. He was not even proceeding along the same line of purpose as these physicists. He was exploring the spiritual and its potential. The scientists are exploring the physical and its potential. I am encouraging this study so that people can have some context for understanding what Hubbard was attempting to describe and make realizable. It just so happens that those in the field of the measurable and observable are running into and beginning to attempt to describe the un-measurable and unobservable essence that Hubbard describes from a completely different approach and purpose. A study of the modern physical approach gives a whole new perspective to Hubbard's entire body of work.

In 1952, Hubbard lectured that Scientologists should not get too caught up in the stories he uses to illustrate concepts, to not get too enamored with the words, because words after all were not the thing – words were simply labels standing for things, some of which defied physical description. Nearly 60 years later, scientist Robert Lanza begins his seminal work, *Biocentrism*, with the same caveat. Lynne McTaggart notes the same concept in *The Intention Experiment*: "In order to describe in words concepts that are generally depicted through mathematical equations, I have had to reach for metaphoric approximations of the truth."

Long before L. Ron Hubbard, Robert Lanza and Lynne McTaggart, Lao Tzu began the *Tao Te Ching* with these words:

The tao that can be told is not the eternal Tao. The name that can be named is not the eternal Name. The unnamable is the eternally real. Naming is the origin of all particular things.

To realize OT (operating or observing and acting outside of the control and undue influence of the physical), it is necessary to transcend the significance of words and constructs. Scientology Inc.'s insistent enforcement of literalness makes that realization impossible. Journalists understand that, witness Janet Reitman and Lynne McTaggart. Scientists understand that, witness Robert Lanza. L. Ron Hubbard clearly understood that. If Scientologists wish to realize the potential of the subject they embrace, they too must come to recognize this.

CHAPTER FIFTEEN

HEREAFTER

Where does Scientology go from here? That is clearly in the hands of those who care about it. I do not purport to have all the answers. The best I can do is to share my perspective. Like everyone else, my views are necessarily molded by my experience. I will relate three major lessons I have learned from those experiences in the outside world since leaving corporate Scientology in 2004. I think they might be of some use to Scientologists for the future. The three lessons are: Integrate or Disintegrate, Evolve or Dissolve, and Transcend or Descend.

Integrate or Disintegrate

One hallmark of the corporate Scientologist that has done more than perhaps anything else to harm the attractiveness of the subject is the assumption of the holier-than-thou attitude. Scientology Inc. drives home at every level, gradiently increasing as one progresses, the idea that a Scientologist is superior to mere mortals and wogs. Some of this is inculcated by Hubbard's writings and lectures. I believe that is partly due to Hubbard feeling the need to keep people involved and engaged when it was particularly tough for one to do so.

During Hubbard's lifetime, Scientologists were continually at risk of losing family, friends, jobs, and even their civil liberties, just by virtue of practicing Scientology. That was due in great part to the established monopoly on mental healing of the '50s and early '60s – driven through the American Medical Association, American Psychiatric Association and American Psychological Association – condemning and organizing aggressive attacks against Scientology. That this was once the case will be made plain in my subsequent book on the movement's history. However, it is still untenable to be associated with Scientology in certain countries, including Germany and France. Hubbard's material consistently regards Scientologists with the attitude that in the light of organized attacks, they ought to take pride for daring to look where others won't.

Hubbard took that defensiveness to another level by becoming increasingly assertive that Scientology is the only workable route to betterment. With that came a growing disdain for other practices and philosophies. It began with psychiatry, spread to psychology and psycho-therapy, and then to other philosophies and religions. By the mid-'60s, firm policies were instituted that effectively forbade the outside study of any other mental, spiritual, or religious philosophy. It was a gradually-growing intolerance, but by the end of Hubbard's life it became sweeping and absolute. By way of example, let us take Hubbard's attitude toward Sigmund Freud and the fields of psychiatry and psychology. Freud was noted by Hubbard as someone to whom "credit in particular is due" at the beginning of his seminal 1951 book *Science of Survival*.

By 1959, Hubbard had toned that acknowledgement down to a condescending tolerance:

Older nineteenth century studies, such as psychology, developed by Wundt in 1879 in Leipzig, Germany; psychoanalysis, developed by Freud in 1894 in Vienna, Austria; and psychiatry, developed through the nineteenth century in Russia, did not necessarily fail, since they provided data which permitted Scientology to begin.

By 1970, Hubbard becomes far more critical:

Any early technology of the human mind was perverted by the University of Leipzig studies of animal fixations of a Prof. Wundt in 1879, who declared man a soul-less animal, subject only to stimulus-response mechanisms and without determinism. Further perversions entered upon the scene in the 1894 libido theory of Sigmund Freud, attributing all reactions and behavior to the sex urge.

Finally, in 1982, Hubbard summed up the contribution of the psychologist, psycho-therapist, and psychiatrist – referred to collectively in Scientology as 'psychs' – in a bulletin entitled *The Cause of Crime*:

There would be no criminals at all if the psychs had not begun to oppress beings into vengeance against society. There's only one remedy for crime – get rid of the psychs! They are causing it!

Corporate Scientologists, trained to abide by all of Hubbard's words literally, believe this without question. Thus, their leader Miscavige currently whips thousands of Scientologists into a virtual frenzy at his annual International Association of Scientologists event – a yearly enactment chillingly reminiscent of Hitler's Nuremburg rallies – by announcing campaigns directed at destroying 'the psychs.' The crowds leap to their feet to give minutes-long standing ovations when Miscavige announces Scientology Inc. funding for the "Psychiatry: Global Retribution" campaign, or the "Psychs: Global Obliteration" plan.

Thus we see what Scientology Inc.'s celebrity spokesman Tom Cruise was referring to when he appeared on the *Today* show and sternly scolded host Matt Lauer with laser-intense certainty: "You are glib. You don't know the history of psychiatry. I do!" And we saw Cruise become the poster boy for Scientology Inc.'s implanted, dysfunctional, superiority complex. Witness Cruise – who claims his "best friend" to be David Miscavige himself – pridefully pronouncing in a viral YouTube video that a Scientologist "knows that he is the only one who can truly help" others, even down to assisting a motorist in distress. What are we to think – that all Highway Patrolmen, Emergency Medical Technicians, even good Samaritans are incompetent, wrong-intentioned people who cannot be trusted?

The first lesson I learned after 27 years on the inside was precisely the opposite. When I left, I moved to deep-south Texas. I had been high profile within, and thought that critics and enemies of Scientology would use my departure to Scientology's detriment. My goal was to disappear. And for three years I was successful. During those three years, I had no contact whatsoever with anyone I had known for the previous entirety of my life. I was a hurt, lonely person. The first thing I noticed was that others noticed that condition. Mind you, these were the lowliest people imaginable, since the county I lived in was perennially one of the three poorest in the nation.

The next thing I noticed was that those lowly 'wogs' cared to do something about my pain. And while they did not have a lot to share, they were only too willing to give the two things they did have: compassion and communication. I noticed that in South Texas people of whatever station or race treat all other people with respect. Men call one another 'Sir' when they meet for the first time or when they casually pass or do simple business. One is automatically granted respect and it is up to one to maintain it. You keep it or lose it by your subsequent conduct, but you start off with their assumption that you deserve it. Where did this come from? I suppose some of it was Christian based, some of it was Mexican-culture based, some of it was Southern-Americana based. Whatever the source, I do know that the compassion and communication that ultimately saved my soul turned out to be inner-city and 'psych' based.

I met Monique Banks in early 2005. The minute she met me, she treated me like a long-lost family member. We have lived together since – we were married in 2010. She had an incredible set of people skills when I met her. They were tolerance, interest, compassion, listening, forgiveness and unconditional love. This woman gave me the space and understanding I needed to decompress, to heal, and to put my life into perspective. It was not till later when I met her father that I would understand where she had learned these skills. Jim Banks is, of all things, a psychotherapist and professor of psychology by profession. Jim is a man's man. He grew up without a father, in the Bronx. He sacrificed his teenage years to serve as father to his four younger brothers. He then served his country in the jungles of Vietnam as a United States Marine. Besides the qualities I already mentioned that Monique displayed, I learned that he taught his children four important lessons.

First, don't ever play the victim – it is the most painful and unrewarding route one can choose, and if played too long will make you a victim for good. Two, remember that you cannot control the way that other people act, but you can always control the way you react to them, and the way you act yourself. Three, if you want to get better and more competent, then choose to associate with friends who are better and more competent than yourself (clearly impossible for one who believes he is superior to the rest). Four – and most importantly – remember that no matter what the question, the answer is 'love.' Ironically, Jim and Monique both naturally, and without effort, exemplified the best qualities that I believe Scientology can help one develop. Jim, despite his profession alone rendering him a 'cause of crime' in the eyes of Scientology Inc., had no problem understanding my description of Scientology. In fact, he agreed with just about everything I told him about it.

Spending time with my new family has taught me that the goals of Scientology are not monopolized. It taught me that there are other means to achieve those goals, and people were exemplifying that in their conduct in the world. This lead to a curiosity about how society and philosophy and the study of the mind had evolved during my years within the machine. I read and read and read some more. The more I read, the more I saw Scientology as aligning with, agreeing with, and potentially having tools that could help with other bodies of wisdom and routes to happiness and realization. I also began to see more clearly how Scientology Inc. had alienated and segregated itself from the rest of society, leaving the world at large with the inclination to steer clear of Scientology.

I never preached Scientology to Monique. But, the subject arose many times, when she would ask me about a good quality in me that she had noticed, which I would attribute to some aspect of Scientology. On three occasions I used simple Scientology techniques to prevent illnesses from taking hold of Monique's body. This increased her curiosity. The more she learned of Scientology from me, the more she considered that it aligned with what she knew to be good, healing, and empowering.

As we learned more of each other, I found that beneath Monique's courage, strength and wisdom she carried hurt and despair like everyone else. She reached for auditing and I provided it. I audited her up the Bridge, through the Grades and Dianetics to Clear. But I audited her up the Bridge with absolutely none of the Black Dianetics additives that have been detailed throughout this book. No attempts were made to have her believe anything, no effort was made to control her behavior and life, nothing was done to get her to view people in any other way than the way she saw appropriate to view them. My goal was solely to help her to recover more of herself, to assist her to take off those synthetic personality jackets that didn't belong to her inherently and were making her uncomfortable – just as Hubbard prescribed when he spoke directly of the actual auditing technology. Though I had audited many dozens of people in my time within Scientology Inc. (including virtually all of its A-list VIPs), it was only during my auditing on the outside that I began to truly appreciate the power of the technology of Scientology.

There was no limit to the effectiveness of Scientology when it was offered and delivered with the sole, unadulterated intent to service and to help. It was completely acceptable and understandable to people when it was not marketed, sold, or covertly forced upon them. It enhanced and reinforced the good lessons that people learned from any number of sources, when it was not used to dissuade people from listening to or learning from other sources. After another three years of delivering Scientology on the same basis to former members of Scientology Inc. and to people new to the subject altogether, those observations have been further validated.

Scientology works wonderfully when it integrates with society, civilization, and the philosophies and religions of others. Scientology harms when it seeks to segregate from society, civilization, and the philosophies and religions of others. If Scientologists do not learn to integrate, they will disintegrate as a potential meaningful influence.

If corporate Scientologists cannot wrap their wits around thinking conceptually with the subject and integrating with society, but instead feel they must continue to act robotically, only according to literal commands of L. Ron Hubbard, then a good start for them would be to aspire to live literally by this central tenet of Hubbard's: "A being is only as valuable as he can serve others."

If one truly attempted to live up to that maxim, he or she might begin to see the light. To Scientologists who can think conceptually and have not cut themselves off from the fruits of observation, you might appreciate the tree from which that branch grew:

What is a good man but a bad man's teacher? What is a bad man but a good man's job? If you do not understand this, you will get lost, however intelligent you are. It is the great secret. — Lao Tzu, Tao Te Ching

Evolve or Dissolve

During my three-year hiatus from communication with any Scientologists, I worked with a man named John Kelley as a writer and editor for his alternative newspaper in Corpus Christi. John is a retired cognitive-behavioral therapist. One day I asked him to describe cognitive-behavioral psychology to me. He said that the therapist guides the patient to review his past, in order to assist him to come to realization (cognition) about his own behavior. The central idea is that a person's behavior can only be changed for the better when the individual self-determinatively recognizes the need for it, and decides to do so himself. The therapist does not invalidate (chastise), or evaluate (tell the patient how to think about himself). Instead he simply guides the person to look, so that the patient may come to cognition. In short, John described the heart and soul of the Scientology auditing process, probably better than I had heard any corporate Scientologist attempt to do so in the past. Comparing my discussions with John to the fevered anti-psych rallies of Scientology Inc. got me to thinking about evolution.

Scientology culture has become so "creationist" in thinking as to be as intolerant and blind to the idea of evolution as the most far-out evangelical cult. After 27 years on the inside, I did not fully recognize that fact until I read Ken Wilbur's *A Brief History of Everything*. Wilbur very intelligently treats the subject of how humanity, culture and civilization have evolved, and continue to. Wilbur does not write about Darwinism, fossils, apes and genetics. He writes about the changes we as thinking people go through every day, and their cumulative effects on the world community over years, and even centuries. Like Hubbard, Wilbur's thinking goes so far outside the box he must create new constructs and even nomenclature to describe the concepts he offers. An honest study of that book would startle a Scientologist. What Wilbur discovers and shares from a philosophical perspective aligns with Scientology as closely as the quantum physicists' discoveries noted in the last chapter. The indirect validations of Scientology in his chapters dealing with spiritual and philosophical evolution are remarkable, particularly when one sees there are no mentions of the subject, and no indication the author has any familiarity with Scientology.

Ironically, while *A Brief History* to me lends a validation to Scientology technology, the organizations of corporate Scientology and the culture it has spawned fit squarely into Wilbur's description of Earth's Dark Ages of stunted and regressed evolution. Those were the times when the church punished and tortured intellectual and scientific renegades who dared to explore outside of – and thus potentially make discoveries contrary to – church doctrine.

Comparing my experience in corporate Scientology to my experience outside of it, and measuring both of them up to accounts and evidence of how philosophy, religion, psychology, and self-help have evolved over the past 60 years, it became apparent to me that Scientology Inc. is not only ignorant of the evolution of thought on Earth, it is fighting it. It is as absurd as Don Quixote's tilting at windmills. But it is far sadder than the story of the man from La Mancha. Quixote's fantasy did not visit much harm upon a lot of others. Scientology Inc. is betraying its own people and the philosophy it purports to hold a monopoly on by, among other things, condemning others who are attempting to evolve.

Where did behavioral-cognitive psychology get the idea that the only effective change could come from within the patient? Certainly not from Scientology – that would be the last place targets of corporate Scientology would look for answers. Perhaps it got it from the same place Hubbard did: Eastern thought. In a 1954 lecture, aptly titled *Scientology: Its General Background*, Hubbard let his people in on how he developed Scientology auditing. Quoting from early Buddhist literature, he explained some of Scientology's bedrock principles:

> *And that is simply this (this is from the Dhammapada): "All that we are is the result of what we have thought. It is founded upon our thoughts; it is made up of our thoughts." Interesting, isn't it? The next verse, you might say, is "By oneself evil is done; by oneself one suffers. By oneself evil is left undone; by oneself one is purified. Purity and impurity belong to oneself; no one can purify another." Well, it's just as you say: You can't grant beingness to the preclear and overawe him; you've got to have him working on self-determinism or not at all, if you wanted to give that any kind of an interpretation. In other words, you've got to restore his ability to grant beingness or he does not become well. And we know that by test.*

As covered throughout this book, those bedrock principles, which serve as the magic that Scientology can be when in well-intentioned hands, have been shattered by corporate Scientology practices which add up to the crippling of self-determinism. And during the decades it took to reverse Scientology practices so thoroughly, traditional mental health practices apparently have adopted some of the same universal truths Scientology is predicated upon. Evolution has thus left Scientology behind. That is not because evolution or the psychological arts and sciences have discriminated against Scientology. It is because the monopoly Hubbard once warned Scientologists against allowing to arise has steered Scientology against evolution. Scientology has become that which it so forcefully resisted. Meanwhile, that which it continues to resist no longer even exists. If

Scientologists do not learn to evolve, their vitality will continue to dissolve.

Transcend or Descend

The Scientology Bridge above Clear as authored by L. Ron Hubbard consists of eight OT levels.

Notwithstanding that fact, at the January, 1986 L. Ron Hubbard funeral event we touched on in Chapter 12, Pat Broeker announced that OT 9 and OT 10 were fully written up by Hubbard and were ready for release. That was a blatant lie.

Twenty years later, David Miscavige told a collection of elite Scientology contributors that L. Ron Hubbard had written up OT 9, OT 10, OT 11, OT 12, OT 13, OT 14 and OT 15. That was a whopping lie. The last OT level L. Ron Hubbard ever wrote up was OT 8. Then he died.

Pat Broeker used the threat of never turning over the alleged OT 9 and OT 10 in an effort to get Miscavige to allow him to exercise control in Scientology Inc. I was a part of three separate forcible search-and-seizures Miscavige directed in order to get at the alleged OT 9 and 10 at Broeker hideouts. Each time we came up empty-handed, and finally concluded there were no such things. This was validated by the senior technical officer of Scientology since L Ron Hubbard's death, one Ray Mithoff. Mithoff audited Hubbard during his final week of life. Mithoff acknowledged in my presence that Hubbard had nothing intelligible to say about any levels that might exist above OT 8, let alone gave any indication that anything had been written up about them.

These horrendous big lies, growing in magnitude as years rolled by, are the continuing creation of the religious con played out through the ages, so well described in Paine's *Age of Reason*.

For those who have honestly accomplished OT 8, it makes perfect sense. After all, at OT 8 Hubbard seeks to guide an individual toward a state or condition of no longer having the slightest attention devoted to past identities, any aspect of the past, introversion or regression. At that level, there wouldn't be even a remote desire for or inclination toward introspective processes or practices of any kind.

A number of people who had completed OT 8 have come to me, hoping that I could give some inside scoop on where Hubbard said it went from there. My response is usually along the lines of: "Please do not invalidate yourself and Hubbard so. Do you think he was cruel enough to build the Bridge to a place where, when you've reached the apex, you are so ill-equipped to move on that you must cling to the guard rail, waiting for some priest to prescribe your every step? Do you feel so vulnerable and weak that you cannot step out on your own and begin to walk your own walk toward higher plateaus?"

I sometimes share the following account of a Zen Buddhist practitioner's colloquy with Zen master Xuedou:

Someone asked Xuedou, "As it is said, 'the road beyond is not transmitted by any of the sages.' Where did you get it?" Xuedou said, "I thought you were a Zen practitioner."

Some express disbelief that Hubbard would not have published something that explicitly let the world know that OT 8 was the end. First, this is not surprising to me. Hubbard was perpetually exploring and prolifically publishing the results of his findings, throughout his life. I would have expected him to be exploring to the end, and if he died before he found anything worthy of publication during his elderly ventures, then the last thing he published would be the last thing he found worthy of publication. Second, if one thinks that OT 8 is the end simply because it is the ultimate attainment on the Scientology Bridge, then from the very beginning one wasn't pursuing the same ends Hubbard was.

To feel or act as if one needed to be the recipient of more knowledge or more effect, then one would have fallen into the trap Hubbard himself warned that formal education had created to sabotage the entire field of philosophy:

> *I hope no man ever falls into that trap because it blocked human thought and human progress. Philosophy became completely abandoned as a subject…and even at this moment they still give a Doctor of Philosophy degree in universities which demands only this of the student: that he know what philosophers have said. Now, that is incredible. If you had a Doctor of Philosophy, you would expect that Doctor of Philosophy to be able to philosophize. The professors of those courses would just be shocked beyond shock if you dared come in and infer that the end and goal of their students should be the production of philosophy. No sir, that's how you keep a society static.*

I have seen subjectively and objectively that this is precisely the product produced by corporate Scientology. They create people who have devoted their entire adult lives to studying and auditing to achieve the ability of 'knowing how to know' (the very definition of Scientology), only to wind up feeling lost, abandoned, and powerless to do anything except to slavishly kowtow to a fascist regime, in hopes it will dispense the next carrot of wisdom.

And so the corporate Scientologist never learns to walk the walk. Instead, he learns to stand compliantly in leg shackles and talk the Scientology Inc. talk.

One who has reached the top in Scientology has two choices: transcend or descend. One can descend down into the mire that corporate Scientology has become. That entails adopting the sickly 'victim' jacket, since a hallmark of a corporate Scientologist is the certainty that until certain people, ideas and even fields of study are exterminated, Scientology can never achieve its aims. It means covertly being a victim while asserting with great energy that you are quite the opposite, the totally-certain superhero who is part of the elite group with the only answer, and thus possess carte blanche with which to forward that group by any means necessary. It includes behaving in a compliant, other-determined fashion, so as to avoid getting into trouble and tarnishing one's image and status. Because in Miscavige's world, image and status have become everything.

Or one can choose to transcend. Transcend with your developed insight and ability to observe and think for yourself. Maybe even use what you know to help others ascend and transcend. For me, that has included using Scientology to help others remove those jackets that keep them weighted to serious, painful lives. Each auditing session I deliver – at whatever level of the Bridge – not only results in cognitions (enlightenments) for the preclear, it also results in cognitions on my part. I continue to study and find and use many other writings, from various sources, that might work more directly to move a particular individual on up a little higher from where he or she might stand. That study also brings about a greater appreciation of what is right and workable and recognition of what is wrong and unworkable about Scientology. But I am not saying that is your calling, purpose, or path to greater heights. Only you can determine what that is.

CHAPTER SIXTEEN

PURPOSE

I began this book with something that I might have provided to Jason Beghe. I am ending this book with something that Jason definitely provided to me. When Jason visited me in 2008, he gave me a copy of the book *Man's Search for Meaning*, by Viktor Frankl. After reading it, I reckoned that it must have had a great deal of influence on the creation of Scientology. It was first published in 1946, just a couple of years before Hubbard first began disseminating tracts on Dianetics. Hubbard never acknowledged the author. Perhaps the parallels were due to the oft-repeated phenomenon in human history where two geniuses discover the same thing at around the same time, in two entirely separate, distant locales. In either event, the central discovery and premise of this little book is the same as the only secret L. Ron Hubbard ever shared publicly about the upper reaches of his OT Level research.

In 1969, and again in the early '80s, Hubbard noted in published works that upper OT level research, above and beyond anything ever published on OT Levels, was all about a thing called purpose. In 1969, he wrote that the clarification and rekindling of a being's basic purpose in life could empower that person to overcome any conceivable obstacles. He wrote that the rehabilitation of purpose "could practically revitalize the dead."

Viktor Frankl was a psychiatrist who was imprisoned in Nazi concentration camps for three years, as a Jew. Only one out of every 28 prisoners survived the Nazi prison experience. Frankl survived not only the notorious Auschwitz and Dachau prisons, but other camps as well. When Frankl was first interned, it so happened he was researching the role and power of purpose in the lives of individuals. It turned out that his imprisonment allowed him to complete that research and find the key to survival and life. It was only when he had lived through the most horrid human conditions imaginable that he fully realized just how he, and only one of every 28 others, made it out alive. He noted that the common denominator was that each of the survivors were driven by such a strong purpose to achieve something meaningful that they withstood that which 27 other fellow human beings perished under.

Frankl could find no other explanation for the serial miracles he witnessed. These included watching one man out of hundreds in a particular cell block failing to succumb to a disease outbreak that took every other life present. That included unexpected, inexplicable acts of mercy being performed by hardened, otherwise sadistic Nazi guards. The only thing that set apart the one from the other 27 was a purpose of such clarity and import to that individual that no disease, no cruelty, no torture, no holocaust could stop its achievement. Frankl recounted his experience, his conclusions, and a methodology for finding and rehabilitating purpose in *Man's Search for Meaning*. Frankl noted that each individual's purpose was unique, and that some were surprisingly simple. On one hand, Frankl himself was saved by his overriding purpose to find the meaning of life and share it with the rest of humanity. Another prisoner's sole, overriding purpose was to re-unite with a particular loved one. Frankl noted that one cannot instill such a strong purpose in an individual. Each person has to find it himself. But when he does, that purpose can overcome matter, energy, space, time and life attempting to extinguish the life that is driven by that individual purpose.

Scientology – at many levels – can assist a person to clarify and rehabilitate his basic, driving purpose in life. There was even a study course Hubbard developed late in his life, designed to assist a person to find that purpose. But, as with virtually all of the Scientology Bridge, that course was perverted by using it to dictate to the individual what purpose he ought to settle upon as his or her own.

I close this book with a short chapter on purpose because I believe Hubbard, the Scientology founder, and Frankl, the psychiatrist, struck upon a common truth that all of humanity can gain something from. It wasn't a particularly new idea. Some 2,500 years before Hubbard and Frankl, Siddhartha Gautama is said to have advised,

Your purpose in life is to find your purpose and give your whole heart and soul to it.

No one has a monopoly on the concept. But Frankl and Hubbard put it into more modern terms, with methods which, when applied, helped people to realize it. That is not to say that other methods created through the ages do not also contribute to that realization.

However, of this I am fairly certain: the degree to which Scientology helps people to find and pursue their inner callings will determine its relevance, longevity and ultimately its value.

MOVING ON UP A LITTLE HIGHER

You can learn more about the independent Scientology movement and about corporate Scientology at my blog Moving On Up A Little Higher:

markrathbun.wordpress.com.

Printed in Great Britain
by Amazon.co.uk, Ltd.,
Marston Gate.